CLUBLAND'S HIDDEN TREASURES

CLUBLAND'S HIDDEN TREASURES

BY

SAM ALDRED

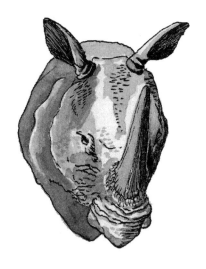

First published in 2020

ISBN: 9798675253821

Dedicated to the memory of

PETER KRAUS

(1968 ~ 2020)

A clubbable American

CONTENTS

SECTION TWO ~ PROVINCIAL CLUBS

PREFACE

This book is intended to be read as a light-hearted romp through Clubland rather than as a work of serious scholarship. "Dates", said Harriette Wilson, "make stories dry and ladies nervous"; their use here is strictly limited. I hope, however, that I have got my facts straight. I have drunk deeply from the existing literature, especially the peerless original edition of Anthony Lejeune's *The Gentlemen's Clubs of London*, several of the more venerable overviews of Clubland, and those histories produced by individual clubs. But I have drawn equally from my time spent in the bars and coffee rooms of Clubland. Above all else, this book has been a joy to research and to write, inspired by my deep affection for this subject. I only hope that this is evident to the reader.

FOREWORD

Clubs are full of precious old relics. Some may be found in the library after lunch and, if prodded and poked, will respond with a kick of limbs and an "unhand me this instant, you elf!" Other objects are inanimate and, as Sam Aldred shows us in this merry little volume, they can reward examination. An ivory inkwell here, a delicate long-case clock there, a deft water-colour or the page from the candidates' book when Kipling was put up for membership and the page was almost completely blackened by scratchy nibs eager to recommend his acceptance.

A favourite item at my own club, the Savile, is a writing desk which was bought with proceeds from the will of Frank Maude, a loyal valet who served the club through the first part of the twentieth century. Clubs belong as much to their staff as they do to their members.

Not all our prizes must be old. Recently the Savile was presented with a new light-shade by its friends in the Flyfishers' Club. This is made of numerous, small, gold-coloured fish which glisten and sway in the draught, like minnows in a stream. That it hangs over a back staircase and may occasionally go unnoticed by passers-by is not the point. Its craftsmanship carries honour and truth and it is there to compensate the leisurely eye.

Clubs are places where the imagination can stray, where delight can dawdle. They are oases of privilege, yes, but not the privilege of class swank or "networking" connections. The average London club membership today has less establishment power than a gathering of personnel managers at a public-sector conference in Milton Keynes. The privilege offered by clubs is the chance to sink into one of those ox-blood leather armchairs mentioned by the Rev Aldred, soak up your surroundings and inhale an hour or so of congenial otherness, far from life's mad cartwheel.

Quentin Letts

The Savile Club

ACKNOWLEDGEMENTS

I owe a debt of gratitude to all those club secretaries, chairmen, librarians, historians, and archivists who have assisted me in my research.

Just as much "research" has taken place informally at many a club table, and I am grateful to those clubmen and clubwomen who have invited me into their home-from-homes to share their stories and their wine.

I thank those dear friends who have proofread my manuscript and offered their advice. I am indebted to my sister-in-law/illustrator, Buffy, for using her considerable talents to beautify this volume. Thank you to my fellow Savilian, the indefatigable Quentin Letts for writing the foreword. Finally, I thank my wife, Helen, for allowing me to scuttle off to London every few months on my "research trips". Now I shall have to find some other excuse.

INTRODUCTION

This is a book about clubs, and about the treasures within those clubs.

Perhaps we ought to begin by defining our terms.

By "clubs" I do not mean the sticky discotheques frequented by hormonal teenagers, nor the tool used for dispatching seal pups, but the sort of establishment which was known in less enlightened times as a "gentlemen's club".[1] The great majority of these clubs are clustered around the St James's and Mayfair districts of London, but they may also be found scattered across the United Kingdom. They are outposts of conviviality in an antisocial age.

This is the realm which the Victorians christened Clubland. It conjures images of leather armchairs and suet puddings, and viscounts in hairy tweeds snoring assertively in empty libraries. Clubland is an archetypally English invention. It is shaped by the Englishman's quiet amiability, his love of belonging,

---

[1] The term "gentlemen's club" has a quite different meaning on the other side of the Atlantic. This became clear to me whilst lunching at a country club in Virginia with a highly respectable nonagenarian. I shall not make the same mistake twice.

his horror of change, and his class snobbery. It is an irony lost on Americans that the grander the clubhouse, the more middle class the club.

The origins of Clubland lie in the coffee houses of Regency England. These early gatherings tended to be bohemian and aristocratic. Brooks's (founded in 1764) has been described as "almost excessively ducal". Brooks's, White's, and Boodle's – London's oldest clubs – remain among the most exclusive. The early flicker of bohemianism has long since been extinguished; though it blazes brightly in other corners of Clubland.

It was in the mid-nineteenth century that Clubland attained its maturity, when – in the words of Harry Flashman – "the age of the Corinthian, the plunger, and the dandy was giving way to that of the prig, the preacher, and the bore." First came the clubs catering for soldiers and diplomats returning from far flung outposts of empire. Then clubs for artists, thinkers, and money-makers began to spread like marmalade across the face of the West End. Huge buildings filled with every modern convenience were erected for every conceivable sort of association. By the ascent of

Edward VII, a solidly clubbable monarch, Clubland was in full bloom.

In common with many Victorian institutions, Clubland stagnated in the second half of the twentieth century. With diminishing returns and cavernous clubhouses to maintain, some clubs amalgamated, bringing two distinct memberships into a marriage of convenience. When the Bath and the Conservative clubs united in 1950, the resulting Frankenclub was nicknamed the Lava-Tory. Many other clubs disappeared altogether. By the 1970s Clubland had reached a nadir. Clubs were incorrigibly uncool. They were the anti-hip, man.

Yet neither the fabness nor the grooviness of the 1970s could deal Clubland a knockout thump. It emerged from that decade smaller and less confident of its place in British society, but it survived. Speaking generally, Clubland today is on firmer footing. The food has improved and the members are younger than in recent decades. Some regional clubs continue to struggle, but in London at least Clubland has regained something of its old swagger.

This is Clubland. What of its "treasures"?

When Saint Lawrence was asked by the pagan prefect of Rome to hand over the treasures of his church, the holy man presented not silver chalices and embroidered vestments but his parishioners. Lawrence was martyred for his little joke by being grilled over an open flame. In a similar manner, more than one club secretary responded to my inquiries by suggesting that the real treasure was to be found amongst the membership. "Oh, you must write about Lord So-and-So, he's such a hoot!" Perhaps you will think me soft, but instead of reaching for my matches I responded to these proposals by politely restating my initial request.

The treasure-troves of Clubland have been expanding steadily for three centuries. The earliest clubs commissioned arcane artefacts for ceremonial purposes. The Society of Dilettanti, whose spectacular pictures now hang in Brooks's, began to meet in 1732. In its early years, whenever a gentleman was elected to membership the president donned a toga and admitted the postulant whilst sitting on a throne of crimson velvet. The club's treasures include a ballot box carved to resemble a Greek temple, with the ballot balls deposited between the open legs of the female figure of Justice; and an ornamental casket of

Honduran mahogany and ivory known as the Tomb of Bacchus. This latter piece is in effect an elaborate piggy bank, used to store the society's dinner money. Both *objets d'art* are still displayed when the Society gathers for its extremely convivial dinners.

Since these pioneering days the clubs of Great Britain have continued to accumulate both priceless works of art and peculiar bits of tat. There are quite as many examples of the latter as of the former. Witness the story of Major Hope-Johnstone at the Pelican Club (long since defunct), who found himself so mired in gambling debts that he was driven to sell his fine set of moustaches and beard, of which he was inordinately proud, to Lord Esme Gordon for the sum of five pounds. Lord Esme removed Hope-Johnstone's facial fluff with a pair of scissors, mounted his quarry on purple velvet, and displayed it in the clubhouse beside the other sporting trophies. The Pelicans were always a boisterous bunch. On one occasion a member was accused of having tossed a boar's head at a peer of the realm, sending him crashing into the fireplace. "Nonsense!" the defendant protested. "I've thrown nothing but jelly all evening."

Clubmen may throw food, but they do not throw stuff away. If something has been in a clubhouse for long enough then it will be there until the last syllable of recorded time. It does not matter how unfashionable a painting may be, or how gruesome a piece of taxidermy, for it is a holy relic and to remove it would be a form of sacrilege. This inventory of ephemera, the legacy of institutional longevity, reminds the current member that he stands on the shoulders of lofty men, part of a heritage greater than himself.

Clubland's Hidden Treasures takes its readers on a tour of these private collections and plucks out the best bits. We shall see portraits, punchbowls, weapons, writs, beds, books, and curiosities which are less easily categorised. We will discover treasures dredged from the ocean floor, seized in battle, shot on safari, and made behind bars. Our cast of characters includes

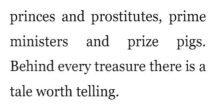 princes and prostitutes, prime ministers and prize pigs. Behind every treasure there is a tale worth telling.

Ring the bell for a large brandy and read on to discover *Clubland's Hidden Treasures*!

A NOTE

A note regarding the structure of the book. Rather than trundling through the clubs alphabetically, or by date of foundation, I thought we might take a virtual walking tour of Clubland. We begin in St James's Square, where a cluster of clubs nestle beside the London Library and the Cypriot embassy. Walking out onto Pall Mall we are faced with the grandest parade of clubs in the world. We shall visit each in turn before turning right onto St James's Street and the birthplace of Clubland. After a quick diversion to Belgravia and Knightsbridge we will stroll into Mayfair, and head finally to the bohemian fringes of Clubland in Soho and Chelsea. The provincial clubs are huddled together at the end. This is intended neither to dismiss them as an afterthought, nor is it a case of saving the best until last. It simply helps with the organising principle. Finally, I feel I should offer an apology to anyone unhappy that his or her own club has not been included; it can only be because I have not had the opportunity to visit. I await my invitation.

The Rev'd Sam Aldred
The Savile Club
September 2020

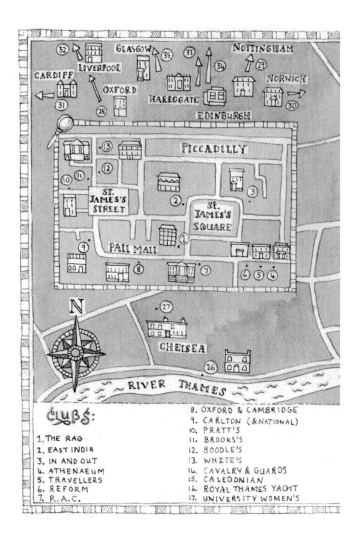

CARDIFF
LIVERPOOL
GLASGOW
NOTTINGHAM
NORWICH
OXFORD
HARROGATE
EDINBURGH

PICCADILLY

ST. JAMES'S STREET

ST. JAMES'S SQUARE

PALL MALL

N

CHELSEA

~ RIVER THAMES ~

CLUBS:

1. THE RAG
2. EAST INDIA
3. IN AND OUT
4. ATHENAEUM
5. TRAVELLERS
6. REFORM
7. R.A.C.

8. OXFORD & CAMBRIDGE
9. CARLTON (&NATIONAL)
10. PRATT'S
11. BROOKS'S
12. BOODLE'S
13. WHITE'S
14. CAVALRY & GUARDS
15. CALEDONIAN
16. ROYAL THAMES YACHT
17. UNIVERSITY WOMEN'S

A MAP OF CLUBLAND

18. SAVILE (& FLYFISHERS)
19. ORIENTAL
20. BUCK'S
21. BLACKS
22. GARRICK
23. BEEFSTEAK
24. NATIONAL LIBERAL (& SAVAGE)
25. FARMERS
26. LONDON SKETCH
27. CHELSEA ARTS
28. FREWEN
29. NOTTINGHAM
30. NORFOLK
31. CARDIFF & COUNTY
32. LIVERPOOL ATHENAEUM
33. HARROGATE
34. NEW
35. GLASGOW ARTS

25

SECTION ONE

LONDON CLUBS

1

THE ARMY AND NAVY CLUB (THE RAG)

NELL GWYNN AUGMENTABLE MINIATURE

Things in the Army and Navy Club are not always as they seem. Take the clubhouse. The current structure was built in 1964 and from the street it looks like a filing cabinet; but once inside it is clear that this new wineskin contains a most agreeable vintage. The Army and Navy Club was founded in 1837, and the two centuries of militaria displayed on its walls proclaims a distinguished heritage. Alongside the souvenirs of battles fought and honours won are a few less expected treasures. There is the mounted head of a fully grown male kudu believed to have been shot in Somaliland in 1927, whose misshapen horn pierces right though its brow.[2] This poor creature is complemented by an Emperor Penguin brought back from Scott's Antarctic expedition. It is quite the little menagerie. Members may be heard toasting "the Emperor" after dinner, though not within earshot of any Frenchmen.

The Army and Navy Club is better known by its nickname, "The Rag". In its early years, the club was popular with officers who purchased their commission with little intention of honest service, and who spent their time swelling about London and causing trouble. One such rascal was Captain Billy Duff. Duff was a drinker and a gambler, who whiled away his hours in a low establishment known as the Rag and Famish. Duff was dismissed in the *United Services Gazette* as "one of those feather-bed soldiers who enter the Army solely for the purpose of wearing a red coat and being dubbed 'Captain'." Stumbling into the Army and Navy Club late one night after a disastrous evening at the

---

[2] A recent examination has revealed that the horn was manipulated posthumously into its current bizarre position.

gaming tables, Duff demanded something to eat. He was presented with some meagre fare, a shrivelled chop and a couple of sausages perhaps, which he shoved away in disgust, proclaiming it to be a "Rag and Famish affair". Those members present were greatly amused, and Duff capitalised on his joke by producing buttons featuring a ragamuffin gnawing on a bone. These were for many years worn by members with their evening dress. A few examples are retained for posterity.

Duff, who died in disgrace, and in Versailles, in 1855 is not the only dissolute character with a connection to the Rag. Several of the more exotic items in the club's collection relate to Nell Gwynn, the Restoration actress, notorious strumpet, and mistress of Charles II. Gwynn was a true celeb in the modern sense, with a tabloid-worthy rags-to-riches backstory and a steamy sex life. The Rag possesses a full-length nude of Nell in the guise of Venus, which was once the cause of some friction between members. One faction thought that it was obscene and should be relegated to a back staircase. The other thought that it was obscene and should be hung in a prominent spot, where it could be enjoyed as widely as possible. The second faction gained the ascendency and the picture now hangs in the smoking room.

A silver fruit knife, dated to 1680, was given as a gift to Nelly by the Merry Monarch. This delicately engraved object may have been an homage to her humble origins as a fruit seller in the theatres of London.[3]

The most interesting of these trinkets is a miniature portrait painted in oils on a copper base roughly 3 ½ by 2 ½ inches in size. It is said to have been worn by Charles II as a token of his affection for the woman whom Samuel Pepys extolled as "pretty, witty Nell". This is no ordinary miniature. It is designed to be augmented with a selection of clear mica overlays, each of which is painted with a different costume. This ingenious design, like later paper dolls, would have enabled the Randy Royal to play dress-up with his mistress. It is one of only about forty such miniatures of any design known to exist. The most likely explanation is that the overlays represent different roles from Nell's career. Curiously, however, they feature a mixture of male and female garments, including clothing for parts which Nell never seems to

---

[3] In Restoration comedy, a fruit-seller was sometimes used euphemistically to mean a prostitute.

have played. The nun's habit is a particular favourite in the Rag. One can imagine that Charles would also have enjoyed this irony, particularly as his long-suffering wife was a devout Roman Catholic.

Why does the Rag have this little collection of Nellobilia? Amusingly, it is all based on a misunderstanding. The old story is that the clubhouse stands on the site of Nell's home. As Pennant describes it, "not having the honour to be on the Queen's establishment, she was obliged to keep her distance at her house in Pall Mall". More recently this theory has been debunked; Nell's house was actually further along Pall Mall at no.79. Because she had insisted on a freehold, it remains the only house on the south side of that street which is not held on a Crown lease. The redoubtable Captain Firebrace (with such a name how can he have been anything other than redoubtable?), in his history of the Rag regrets that it is "an ungrateful task to demolish a long standing tradition", but demolish it he must. Well indeed, but at least the tradition has resulted in this admirable little collection.

As we began by observing, things at the Rag are not always what they seem. The other surviving examples of these augmentable miniatures come in two designs, one male and one female. The male figure is undoubtedly Charles I. They may have formed part of the campaign to promote Charles as a martyred saint following his execution in 1649. This has led historians to posit that the female figure is actually his wife, Henrietta Maria. This makes more sense of the royal and religious costumes, for unlike Nell Gwynn she was both a queen and a Roman Catholic. However, all of this rests on conjecture. Only one thing can be said for certain: the woman depicted in this miniature is wearing the most intensely flirtatious expression. Perhaps this portrait does not depict Nell Gwynn, and perhaps she never had any connection to the Rag in the first place. *C'est la vie.* The important thing is that it makes a jolly interesting story, and perhaps that is all that really matters.

2

THE EAST INDIA CLUB

NORTH AFRICAN CHAINMAIL

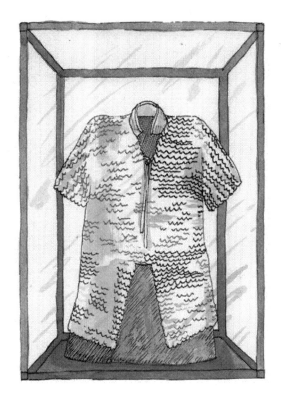

Ask a stranger to describe a typical London club and they will give you something approximating the East India: generously proportioned, of dignified character, and smelling pervasively of leather. This description works for both the clubhouse and its members, known as Eastindiamen.

No. 16 St James's Square had a notable career as a private residence long before the East India took it on in 1849. It was here in 1815 that the Prince Regent was told of the Allied victory at Waterloo. He was settling down to dine with Lord Castlereagh and Lord Liverpool when in burst Major Henry Percy, direct from the field of battle. The Prince Regent was presented with the captured French eagles and dispatches from the Duke of Wellington. It used to be possible to take a drink on the balcony from which he announced the news to the crowd below, but not anymore. Perhaps someone fell off.

For its first hundred years, the East India Club drew its membership from amongst that great army of soldiers, diplomats, traders, and imperial administrators who returned to London from India and across the wider empire with stories to tell and money to spend. When Britain lost its empire, a new source of members needed to be sought, and the East India reinvented itself successfully as a club of many clubs. Today, its full name is the East India, Devonshire, Sports, and Public Schools Club, attesting to the closures and amalgamations which reduced the bounds of Clubland during those dark three decades after the end of the Second World War.[4] As a result of this catholicity, the clubhouse has something of the cornucopia about it, overflowing with the trinkets and treasures of its constituent clubs. This adds character to what could otherwise be a wantonly large and grand building.

Here are three good reasons to visit the East India Club. Firstly, to dine in its stately coffee room, one of the finest in London. Secondly, to take a stroll down the corridor of taxidermy on the first floor, which culminates in the head of an enormous hippopotamus, its mouth fixed in an eternal yawn. It is possible to place one's own head inside the hippo's terrifying maw, which alone is worth the visit to St James's Square. But I would suggest that the best reason to visit the East India Club is to drink a whisky and soda in the American Bar, rebuilt after bomb damage in the 1940s to resemble a half-timbered country pub. There are two notable treasures displayed in this watering hole. One will be dealt with in the next chapter. The other is a jerkin of chainmail – what in Medieval Europe was called a hauberk – presented to the club

---

[4] The Sports Club joined in 1939, the Public Schools Club in 1972, and the Devonshire after it disbanded in 1976. The first two bought a young and hearty membership, and the latter a huge dowry and a certain social cache.

in the early twentieth century by a heroic young member, shortly before his death.

The jerkin was taken at the Battle of Kano in 1903, a decisive victory for the British in Northern Nigeria against the fast-fading Kano Emirate. It was acquired by Captain George Howard Fanshawe Abadie, a dashing colonial administrator and typical Eastindiaman. Abadie cut his teeth in India as an officer in the 16th Lancers, before transferring to Africa in 1897. He soon made a name for himself as a savvy operator. One account gushed:

> [Abadie] began his tour of service by carrying out an enterprise which the High Commissioner described as one of the most brilliant things done in the country, the capture, almost single-handed, of Ibrahim, the ex-Emir of Kontagora... the most powerful and dreaded slave raider among the Fula chiefs, and a man looked upon with superstitious awe by Muhammadans.

The young captain's fame in Northern Nigeria was such that the Emir of Kano offered £500 to anyone who could bring him Abadie's head. No head-hunter was to have the chance, however. Abadie died from fever in 1904, at the age of thirty. His obituary in the *Journal of the Royal African Society* effused that Abadie "was the best type of the soldier-administrator, an embodiment of the 'fair and kindly spirit, bred in our public schools'". Abadie was present at the Battle of Kano as a political officer attached to the British forces. It was here that he acquired the chainmail coat from one of the three hundred Nigerian cavalryman who faced the British that day.

In parts of North Africa, cavalry units continue to wear chainmail into the middle of the twentieth century. The mail jacket now in the East India is typical of that found in Northern Nigeria. Favoured because it was lightweight and did not restrict movement, such armour clearly offered insufficient protection against British firepower.[5]

The wearing of chainmail by certain African armies was a source of fascination to those who faced them on

---

[5] In the Armorers' Hall there is a magnificent suit of armour worn at the Battle of Omdurman, which is riddled with bullet holes from a British maxim gun.

the battlefield, conjuring images of the medieval crusades. In one case this crusading fantasy may have been tinged with truth. In the 1880s and 1890s the British sent troops into Sudan, where they battled the armies of the self-proclaimed reincarnation of the Prophet Muhammed; he took the name Mahdi, meaning "the expected leader". It has been suggested – perhaps implausibly, but only perhaps – that some of the Mahdi's cavalry wore medieval helmets, plate armour, and chainmail, and wielded huge broadswords which were relics of the fourteenth century crusades.

The American Bar of the East India Club is one of the cosiest spots in Clubland. Its tankards and Twiglets conjure the ambience of some sleepy village inn, far away from the great clubhouses of Piccadilly. But few rustic taverns contain a treasure as unexpected as Captain Abadie's bequest to the East India Club. Where else but Clubland could one admire a jerkin of twentieth century African chainmail whilst sipping on a pint of London Pride?

THE ECCENTRIC CLUB

OWL CLOCK

Those of us who read the Old Testament are confronted by the incredible fact of Israel's survival. This perennially unlucky tribe, with its devotion to an unnameable Deity given to smiting his worshippers, survived through exodus, exile, and attempted extermination from pre-history to the present day. I sometimes feel a pang of sadness for those other tribes who appear in the pages of Scripture, and whose memory is lost in the shifting sands of time. What do we know today of the Perizzites or the Girgashites, the Kadmonites and Kenizzites? Those strange and forgotten peoples, the playground bullies of Exodus and Chronicles, appear to us only as footnotes in the history of the Hebrews. So it is with clubs (a tenuous link, certainly, but please do bear with me). The history of Clubland is strewn with the names of long-forgotten and half-remembered clubs. Who still recounts the exploits of the Nimrod, the Fox, the Ladies' Imperial, or the Junior Constitutional?

By every right, the Eccentric should have a place on this list of forgotten clubs, and yet it clings onto life. No longer do the Eccentrics have their splendid Ryder Street Clubhouse. They do not even possess a room of their own in the premises of a larger club, in the manner of the Savage or the Flyfishers.[6] The Eccentrics live a peripatetic existence, meeting between the Savile, the Oriental, and wherever else will give them hospitality. But still they live on. Actually, the Eccentric Club of today is a re-foundation with only a tenuous link to the former club, but this is in the Eccentric spirit. The original Eccentric Club, known variously as the Illustrious Society of Eccentrics, or optimistically as the Everlasting Society of Eccentrics, was founded in 1781, and thrived in various locales until the 1840s. It counted among its

---

[6] As Virginia Woolf very nearly said, "a room of one's own is better than nowt."

members such political luminaries as Lord Melbourne and the eminently clubbable Charles James Fox.

This initial incarnation was extinguished in 1846. The name was used by another group in the 1850s and 60s, but it wasn't until 1890 that the Eccentric experienced a full resurrection, courtesy of a theatrical costumier named Jack Harrison. Harrison gathered around himself a coterie of gentlemen associated with the music hall, and together they adopted the old Eccentric mantle. This vaudevillian influx gave the new Eccentric a rakish, vaguely disreputable feel. If Boodle's and Brooks's sneered at these uncouth upstarts then the Eccentrics winked and cocked a snook back. The Eccentric became one of the jauntiest, most ebullient clubs in all of London, famed for its excellent food and extensive wine-cellars. It was also one of the most generous, applauded for its philanthropic spirit. These twin emphases on fun and duty inspired its motto, *Nil nisi bonum.*

The Eccentric Club adopted as its symbol the night owl, pictured together with a clock-face showing 4am: a reference to the hours kept by the membership. The Eccentric's clubhouse featured several owls, including a scruffy little taxidermied tawny with a wrist-watch clasped in its beak. When the club hit financial difficulties it sold many of its possessions, and after the Eccentric disbanded in 1986 its collection was scattered to the four-winds. However, the Eccentric spirit was not crushed. In a new form, the most famous of these avian objects lives on at the East India Club. This is a replica of a thoroughly eccentric clock dreamt-up by member W.E. Clifford, the original of which had hung above the Owl's Roost Bar in Ryder Street.

The clock-face is gripped in the talons of the Eccentric's totemic night owl, and it is all but useless as a means of telling the time, because not only are the numbers the wrong way round, but it also runs backwards. This inspired one wag to joke, "The Eccentric Club in London with its clock running backwards: I wished they would have me as a member, so I could meet all my old friends again..." The original clock was carved rather splendidly but this was sold-off in 1955, to whom no-one remembers. The clock which hangs today in the American Bar of the East India Club is a smaller, manufactured copy. It was installed in 2006 by a group of former Eccentrics who wanted to preserve some memory of their former existence.

The Eccentric was resurrected once again in 2008. Whether the newest Eccentric Club will fare as well as its previous incarnations remains to be seen. Certainly their ambition of owning their own London clubhouse seems fanciful. Stranger things have happened, however, and one must never underestimate a determined clubman.

Normally I would not trust a gentleman who claims to be an eccentric. Like a woman who calls herself a lady, if it has to be insisted upon then it is almost certainly not true. However, upon its refoundation, the Eccentric Club welcomed as its patron HRH Philip, Duke of Edinburgh. A man regarded as a god by the Tanna Islanders and as a saint by the *Daily Telegraph*, all can surely agree that he is a true eccentric. Under his royal patronage we hope that the Eccentric Club will become more than just another dusty file in the archives of Clubland.

4

THE NAVAL AND MILITARY CLUB

(THE IN AND OUT)

CANNING CLUB MAP

The Naval and Military Club gained its nickname from the prominent signs outside its Piccadilly clubhouse, indicating vehicle entrance and exit gates. When the club relocated to No. 4 St James's Square in 1999, the "In" and the "Out" moved with it, although the venerable monosyllabic commands were retired from their traffic-directing function to retain a purely aesthetic role. Before it became a clubhouse, No. 4 St James's Square had a varied career. Between 1912 and 1942, it was the home of Viscountess Astor, the first woman to sit as a Member of Parliament. The property then was requisitioned by the government and used as the London headquarters of the Free French Forces. In September 1947 it became the home of the Arts Council of Great Britain, and was later used as a division of the High Court. Having been the backdrop for political intrigue, military strategizing, artistic posturing, and legal wrangling, the arrival of the In and Out must have come as a pleasant relief.

The club wears its military heritage lightly. The membership is young and diverse, attracted more by the dining and sports facilities than by the historic service connections. A broadening of the membership beyond soldiers and sailors began in the 1960s, when the In and Out assumed into its flow a number of tributary clubs. These included two historic female clubs, the Ladies' Carlton and the Cowdray, and later the bridge-playing Portland Club. These amalgamations injected new life at a time when many clubs were going the way of all flesh. Two others clubs have retained their independence whilst having full use of the In and Out: the Canning with its South American focus (about which more shortly), and Den Norske Klub, which caters to London-based Norwegians. If one arrives at the In and Out expecting to see retired colonels dozing in dusty parlours, then one should prepare to be disappointed.

Aspects of the club's décor remain distinctly martial. The portraits are of chaps with ruddy faces and lots of ruddy medals. A magnificent display of regimental crests runs up the staircase. Then there is the taxidermied head of an Indian one horned rhinoceros, presented in 1903 by Lieutenant H.B. Firman of the 16th Queen's Lancers. Pound for pound there can have been few more generous bequests in the history of Clubland. One can only imagine how vast and stately the creature must have been when still exhibiting vital signs. How ancient, how *prehistoric*, he appears; and how disgruntled at having been pinned above a staircase in a drizzly metropolis some four thousand miles from home.

Perhaps the loveliest treasure actually belongs to the Canning Club. Founded in 1911 for those with business links to Argentina, it was originally called the Argentine Club and had its own clubhouse at No. 1

Hamilton Place. The club thrived during the Second World War, when it provided a home-from-home for many of the eight hundred Argentine men who volunteered to fight for H.M.'s forces; a little remembered chapter of Anglo-Argentine history. The good times did not last, however, and when Juan Domingo Perón came to power in 1946 he nationalised the Argentine economy and drove out British investors. At this point the Argentine Club wisely shifted its focus onto all of Latin America, and adopted its new name in honour of George Canning, that great supporter of South American independence. After coming to a mutually-satisfying arrangement with the In and Out in 1970, the Canning Club experienced a new lease of life during the Falklands War, when its members helped to establish the South Atlantic Council.

The Canning Room at No. 4 St James's Square is named in honour of the Canning Club; a tangible reminder of that club's presence alongside the In and Out. The room is dominated by a large painted map of the old and new worlds. It depicts the transatlantic trade routes which brought the Argentine Club into existence, executed in an idealised, dreamy style. Whales and giant squid sport in the waters beside tall ships, and exotic birds soar through the air. Cherubs in the top western corner blow galleons laden with precious cargo back to the markets of Europe. A benevolent sun shines its benediction on all this industriousness.

It is not known who painted the map or when; its origins were lost when the Canning joined forces with the In and Out. It was most likely commissioned in the 1930s, as the form of the Spanish crest indicates that it was designed shortly after General Franco came to power. If this is the case then the name of the Canning Club would have been added to the bottom right corner at a later point. This logo is surrounded by several South American staples, including the inevitable llama, a cactus, and a Gringo in poncho and sombrero. When the Canning had their own clubhouse this map hung on the staircase, and a chunk is missing from the bottom where a bannister once ran beneath it. Today it beautifies No. 4 St James's Square, that Tardis-like clubhouse between Jermyn St and Pall Mall, where Anglo-Argentine relations are never anything less than cordial.

5

THE ATHENAEUM

Q' & A' BOOK

The Athenaeum's clubhouse is one of the most recognisable buildings in London; a noble neo-Grecian structure overlooking St James's Park, encircled by a classical frieze and surmounted by a golden statue of the goddess Athene, who looks as though she is conducting a pagan *Urbi et Orbi* for the tourists below. Decimus Burton was only twenty-four when he received the commission, which does rather make one consider one's life choices.

The Ath. was conceived in 1824 by John Wilson Croker, the author, bruiser, and secretary of the admiralty. It was Croker who insisted on installing the frieze on the outside of the building, a copy of the recently acquired Elgin Marbles, at the enormous cost of over £2,000. Other members would have preferred the money to have been spent on cold-storage facilities, inspiring one wag to compose the ditty:

I'm John Wilson Croker,

I do as I please;

Instead of an Ice House

I give you - a frieze!

The first committee included some of the finest minds of that generation, with Michael Faraday in the chair. On the subject of Faraday and chairs, the wheelchair used by the father of electromagnetics is kept in the library on the first floor. The Athenaeum was instituted "for the association of individuals known for their scientific and literary attainments, artists of eminence in any class of the fine arts and noblemen and gentlemen distinguished as liberal patrons of science, literature or the arts." While such men would form the basis of many later clubs, this marked a departure from the more resolutely aristocratic clubs of the eighteenth century, dedicated principally to gambling and consuming heroic quantities of beefsteak.[7]

The Athenaeum soon became known as *the* club to join for the chronically big-brained. Charles Dickens was elected to membership on the same day as Charles Darwin. To date there have been fifty-two Nobel Prize winners amongst the membership, including at least one in each category. As Lejeune comments, "The Athenaeum has a formidable reputation for intellectuality, gravity, deep respectability and episcopacy." There was a time in the early twentieth century when one could hardly move for bishops avoiding their diocese and ignoring their clergy. Surely it is no coincidence that this was a great age for the Established Church. This episcopal quality has not always been popular with other members. Abraham Hayward is said to have complained, "I see the Bishops are beginning to swarm: the atmosphere is alive with them; every moment I expect to find one dropping into my soup." Later, Kipling opined that "coming to the

---

[7] In 1982 the Athenaeum ordered new plate which erroneously recorded the date of the club's foundation as 1724, rather than 1824. All evidence of this error was later destroyed.

Athenaeum is like entering a cathedral between services."

In homage to the Athenaeum's men of letters, our object of interest takes the form of a cloth-bound tome which can be found in the drawing room. Unlike some of the objects in this volume, the interest of which lies in their outward form, this book must be prized open to reveal its pearls of wisdom. This is the Athenaeum's Question Book, a sort of proto-Google in which members pose questions to be answered by their peers. There are no previous volumes; the tradition only began in 1963. It was the brainchild of Miss Penhaligon, the indomitable club librarian, and was no doubt instituted in order to dissuade members from directing their queries at her.

The first entry, by a Mr J.M. Ross, concerns the origins of the game of Nine Men's Morris. This sets the tone admirably for what follows. Some favourite entries include: "What is the Significance of the toad in Sicily?" (A: "They contain the souls of the proud"); "Why do Sumo Wrestlers shave their legs?" (A: "for the pure beauty of it"); and, "Do bananas grow in the USSR?" (A: "No"). Other members have used the book to vent about mundane issues such as the poor quality of the club's napkins, and the disappearance of books from the library. By far the most common entries concern the provenance of literary quotations, and other queries which today could be answered at the press of a button.

Some questions remain unanswered. Others receive a response long after the author has ceased to be troubled by their entry. A question from 1975 asking about the decline in snuff-taking was only answered in 1985, by a member who had been offered some that evening. Some questions are clearly phrased to cause a stir. In 1989 the notorious Fr Brian Brindley asked which nations typified the seven deadly sins. It is prudent not to record the answers suggested by one member for fear of upsetting any Scottish, Iranian, Japanese, French, German, American, or Russian readers.[8]

Sadly, over the last twenty years the Question Book has fallen out of usage; like high street travel agents and pornographic cinemas it has been superseded by the internet. This is a great loss to Clubland. Although

---

[8] This same cleric, Canon Brian Dominic Frederick Titus Leo Brindley, died at the Athenaeum during a seven-course dinner held to celebrate his seventieth birthday. He suffered a massive heart attack between the dressed crab and the *boeuf en croûte*.

there is now an easier way to source answers to one's questions this is surely a case of quantity over quality. I know that I would trust the considered opinion of a perspicacious Athenian over that of a pustulous teenager. Besides, as one member observes, "many surfers of the internet are unclubbable".

6

THE TRAVELLERS CLUB

THE ORLÉANS CABINET

A member of a boisterous provincial club, visiting the Travellers as part of a reciprocal arrangement, might find the atmosphere subdued, even somnolent. There is a convention that members do not talk to each other. Involuntary sneezes are met by lowered newspapers and raised eyebrows. Smiling is punishable by a fine of 30 shillings, or half a dozen lashes with a knotted cord depending on the severity of the infringement. The

Travellers is a refuge from the noise of a busy world. It is – in the parlance of the day – a "safe space" for gentlemen deranged by piped music and commercial radio stations.[9]

'Twas not ever thus. The Travellers Club emerged in the aftermath of the Napoleonic Wars, and is said to have been the bright idea of Viscount Castlereagh, the Foreign Secretary and British Minister Plenipotentiary at the Congress of Vienna. The Congress was notable principally for creating a lasting peace in Europe. The Austrians celebrated by throwing one helluva party. This included a re-enacted medieval joust at which Castlereagh's wife caused a sensation by wearing her husband's diamond-studded Order of the Garter in her hair. Altogether, the British delegation to the Congress drank 10,000 bottles of wine. It was with such conviviality in mind, as well as the spirit of international concord, that the Travellers Club was founded in 1819.

Membership of the Travellers Club is open to any gentleman who has travelled five hundred miles in a

---

[9] The Travellers is said to be the inspiration for the fictional Diogenes Club, co-founded by Sherlock Holmes' brother Mycroft. It was a club for "the most unsociable and unclubbable men in town".

straight line from London. This was a rather more impressive feat in the mid-nineteenth century, and today the club contains few genuine explorers and adventurers, though there is still a strong representation from the FCO. Importantly, the Travellers was also envisaged as a place to show hospitality to visiting dignitaries. The most famous of these honoured guests was Prince Talleyrand, who was a frequenter of the club's whist tables during his autumn years as French ambassador to the Court of St James's. A handrail was installed to enable the octogenarian (and club footed) Talleyrand to heave his way upstairs.[10]

The library of the Travellers is one of the finest rooms in all of London, with its clusters of pale oak pillars and walls of books, all crowned by a cast of the Bassae Frieze. A "metamorphic chair" which folds out into a stepladder dates from 1820 and was part of the club's original furnishings. There is even one of those doors disguised as a bookcase, which seems to be lifted straight from an episode of *Scooby Doo*. This mixture of whimsy and classicism is irresistible. Opposite the

---

[10] Talleyrand's club foot was described by one lover as being "a horse's hoof made of flesh ending in a claw". James Gillray believed it to be an emblem of the French statesman's depravity.

entrance to the library stands the Orléans Cabinet, containing a collection of exquisitely bound volumes. The history of this cabinet is the history of the Travellers Club in miniature. It also has a happy ending and imparts a moral lesson, which is more than can be said about most pieces of furniture.

The story begins on 6th March 1848 with the arrival in England of Louis-Philippe, the deposed King of the French, and his family. In accordance with the founding principles of the Travellers Club, the King's sons were given honorary membership during their years in exile. Like Talleyrand before them, the Orléans princes made excellent use of this hospitality from their bolthole in Twickenham.

In 1859, to show their gratitude, the princes presented the Travellers Club with what has been described as "a suitably majestic example of the Parisian art of book production" in the form of nineteen large folio volumes of the *edition de grand luxe* of Charles Gavard's *Galeries historiques de Versailles*. This was a richly illustrated record of the museum which Louis-Philippe had founded at Versailles to celebrate French history, and in no small part to legitimise his own claim to the French crown. The dedication leaf is signed by Louis-Philippe's grandson, the Comte de Paris (who succeeded theoretically as Louis-Philippe II but never reigned), and three of the King's sons: the Duc de Nemours, the Prince de Joinville, and the Duc d'Aumale.

Such splendid books deserved a splendid home, and Charles Annoott of Bond Street – a cabinet maker of French origin – was appointed to create something worthy of the royal gift. The result was an ormolu-mounted cabinet of English oak in French style, decorated with the *fleur-de-lis* of the house of Orléans. Glazed sliding doors reveal the volumes within. The top of the cabinet folds out to form two leather-lined reading ledges, and a brass plaque records the circumstances behind the donation. The cabinet was given pride of place in the library, where it remained for over a century; a reminder of that increasingly distant age when exiled aristos rubbed epaulettes with sun-scorched explorers in a gilded, fashionable clubhouse.

By the 1970s, things weren't looking so hot. In common with the rest of Clubland, the best days of the Travellers Club had long since passed. Membership was down, fees were up, and the clubhouse required urgent maintenance. In 1975, with Britain in the grip of a double-dip recession, the committee took the difficult decision to sell the Orléans Cabinet in order to raise some funds. It went to an antiquarian bookseller for only £1000. Many within the club were distressed by the decision, and note was taken whenever the cabinet appeared for auction. In 2010 it was seen in Christie's New York, and two years later it popped up at Koller's in Zurich. It was then that the club's secretary decided to strike. A fund-raising campaign was launched and the membership responded enthusiastically. A bid of £61,000 was accepted and in April 2012 the Orléans Cabinet was returned to its rightful home.

The cabinet has been restored to its original condition, and sits once again in its intended corner of one of London's most marvellous rooms. Perhaps fittingly, it has now travelled the five hundred miles required for membership of the club, and then some. I promised you a happy ending. And the moral of the story? Do not sell off the family silver.

7

THE REFORM CLUB

PORTRAIT OF ALEXIS SOYER BY EMMA SOYER

When Jubby Ingrams was discovered late one evening in the gentlemen's lavatories of the Reform Club, relieving herself in a washbasin, she and her friends were asked to leave and never to return. As she was with a party organised by the notoriously acerbic Auberon Waugh, the Reform Club's response to this indiscretion was promptly denounced from Waugh's pulpit in the *Literary Review*. "Every club, I suppose, has its quota of bores and pompous oafs", fumed Waugh. "It is only when they manage to take it over that the dimness really sets in."[11] As ever, Waugh was guilty of exaggeration. The Reform has never been a boring or a pompous club, but it certainly has a serious streak. The Reform Club was founded in 1836 by serious men in order to serve a serious purpose: to nurture the progressive spirit which had succeeded in passing the Reform Act of 1832. Silly girls urinating in sinks did not play even a small part in this noble vision.

The Reform Club grew out of the bitter parliamentary dispute between Whigs and Radicals. It was intended to supersede Brooks's, controlled as that more ancient and aristocratic club was by "loathsome" Whigs, as one Radical wrote, "of hideous sight and pestiferous smell." In due time the Reform would itself be superseded as the home of progressive politics in

---

[11] Not content to sit and carp from the side-lines, Waugh founded his own club – the Academy – which had only one rule: like Plato's Republic, there were to be no poets.

Clubland by the National Liberal Club, but that is a story for another chapter.[12]

Sir Charles Barry's spectacular design for the Reform's clubhouse bears more than a passing resemblance to Michelangelo's Palazzo Farnese. The central feature is a vast central hall, flanked by columns and busts of the great reformers. Barry had intended to leave this space uncovered in the style of an Italian courtyard, but the realities of the English climate necessitated a glass roof be installed; this is constructed from a thousand lead crystal lozenges and is a thing of beauty in its own right.

Despite all of these charms, it was the club's kitchens which garnered the most interest, and ensured that the Reform Club became a place of gastronomic pilgrimage. It is worth emphasising the scale of this achievement, because club cuisine has historically been derided as the sort of nursery food favoured by institutionalised men. (And also, incidentally, by Idi Amin, whose favourite dishes were steak-and-kidney

---

[12] Chapter 26, to be precise. There has never been a club for members of the Labour Party. This is because Labour voters tend to be pubbable rather than clubbable.

pie and chocolate pudding).[13] Bad food was served at even the smartest clubs. Sir Edwin Lutyens was once lunching at Brooks's when he was presented with an unpromising fish dish.

"What on earth is this?" he demanded.

The waiter replied, "A piece of cod, sir."

" – which passeth all understanding!" came the incomparable retort.[14]

The gentlemen of the Reform Club demanded something better, and by Jove they got it, courtesy of an exceptional chef named Alexis Soyer.

Born in 1810 to French Protestant parents, the young Alexis Soyer was destined to enter the ministry until he decided to engineer his expulsion from seminary by ringing the church bells late one night. This might seem like a harmless student prank, but as the bells doubled as the town's fire alarm the stunt roused not

---

[13] Despite having a clubman's appetite, General Amin was *not* a clubbable man.

[14] Some versions of this story have it set in the Athenaeum, which has a well-deserved reputation for unpalatable food. In the 1970s the Ath' employed a chef who lost his ability to taste salt, with the result that his dishes were nauseatingly over-seasoned. Finally, a member, driven beyond the bounds of frustration, marched into the kitchen to remonstrate with the chef, only to be assaulted himself.

only the townsfolk but also the local garrison. Duly freed from the stultifying prospect of a clerical career, Alexis was free to pursue his culinary ambitions. He sailed to England, working at first in the kitchens of aristocratic gourmands. Then, in 1837, the Frenchman took up the role which was to make him famous, as *chef de cuisine* of the new Reform Club.

Joining the Reform shortly after its creation, Soyer was given the opportunity to work in partnership with Charles Barry to transform the clubhouse's basement into a network of kitchens which far surpassed anything else then known in Europe. It quickly became apparent that the young Frenchman was an inspired inventor as well as a whiz with the whisk. The key to Soyer's vision was the careful manipulation of fire, water, gas, steam, and ice to create an efficient and healthy workspace quite unlike the smoky, suffocating kitchens then common in even the grandest houses.

Soyer's kitchens contained banks of innovative temperature-controlled ovens, fish slabs kept cool by running ice water, and steam powered dumb waiters to carry the food up two stories to the main dining room. As one newspaperman gushed, "Heliogabulus himself never gloated over such a kitchen, for steam is here introduced and made to supply the part of man." The kitchens were further ornamented with smaller gadgets of Soyer's own invention, some of which – like plug strainers, and the *cafetière* – would become household staples. The *pieces de resistance* were the two gas stoves which Soyer employed to such estimable effect decades before this technology gained general acceptance.[15] The kitchens were described by one enchanted vicomtesse as being "as spacious as a ballroom... and white as a young bride": one of the wonders of the modern world.

Members and their guests flocked to see the celebrity chef at work in his subterranean kingdom; in 1846 alone Soyer claimed to have received over fifteen thousand visitors. Surely he must be the only employee in Clubland's history to have garnered a mention in every contemporary newspaper account of his club. Indeed, it is no exaggeration to say that Alexis Soyer was Britain's first celebrity chef. He was the first to publish a series of bestselling cookery books; the first to produce branded merchandise; and the first to consciously nurture his public profile. After leaving the Reform in 1850, Soyer went on to design a new sort

---

[15] In 1807, Pall Mall became the first street in London to be lit by gas lamp.

of soup kitchen during the Irish Famine, and invented his "magic stove" for use by the British Army in the Crimea, a variant of which was still being employed in the 1980s. But Soyer is best known for his ground-breaking work in the Reform Club.

The basic structure and organisation of Soyer's kitchen remains in place today, even if many of his innovations have been superseded, and dogs are no longer allowed to roam free. The pastry kitchen is where it was in Soyer's time, as is the potwash. His signature dish – Lamb Cutlets Reform – remains on the menu. Another survival is the chef's office which Soyer built within the kitchen as a vantage point to oversee the whole operation. In Soyer's day it was decorated with pictures painted by Emma, his wife.

Alexis and Emma married in 1837, when she was already gaining a reputation in art circles for her oil portraits. A critic in *The Times* commented, "No female artist has exceeded this lady as a colourist, and very few artists of the rougher sex have produced portraits so full of character, spirit, and vigour." All of these talents are evident in the portrait of her puckish husband which now hangs in the Strangers' dining room. Alexis wears his trademark red beret and broad

Gallic grin, and is eating his favourite dish: truffled chicken.

Emma died whilst pregnant with Alexis' first child. The young mother-to-be was frightened into an early labour during a thunderstorm. By the time help arrived the mother and baby were both dead. Alexis was heartbroken; his wife was only twenty-eight years old. An elaborate monument standing at over twenty feet tall was erected in Kensal Green Cemetery. It contains a cleverly concealed gas flue which fed an eternal flame, designed, of course, by Alexis.

8

THE ROYAL AUTOMOBILE CLUB

THE SIMMS MOTOR CAR

Frederick Richard Simms claimed to have conceived what became the Royal Automobile Club during the "Emancipation Run" of 1896. The Emancipation Run was a cavalcade of some thirty-two motor vehicles – perhaps as many as half of all those in Britain at the time – which made its way from London to Brighton, on a route lined with many thousands of spectators, to celebrate the repeal of the infamous Red Flag Act. This unprecedented spectacle, reported by contemporaries as being both exhilarating and terrifying, might be considered the birth of the motor age in this country. Along with some other enthusiastic motorists, Simms was there from the very start. In fact it was not until the following year that Simms established the Automobile Club of Great Britain (and later Ireland), and not until 1907 that the club was adopted by the petrol-head-in-chief, King Edward VII, at which point it gained a royal prefix and the name that it holds to this day.[16] The so-called "Parliament of Motoring" was now in session.

The RAC clubhouse, an enduring testimony to Edwardian opulence, opened its substantial doors in 1911. The clubmen of Pall Mall were not sure what to make of this new arrival. The reactions of some were laced with snobbery. "I fancy I can see them now", wrote one, "furred, goggled, spare-tired and cigar-smoking, with a crowd of messenger boys and loafers sitting on the mudguards of the cars". Others were cowed into silence; their own clubs were dwarfed by a

---

[16] Although a keen motorist, Edward VII never learnt much about cars. When things went wrong, he would growl at his chauffer, "This should not be!"

club so large that one member compared it to a "bloody great railway station".

Palatial is far too often the adjective which writers reach for when attempting to conjure the image of a consciously and conspicuously grand building. To write that the London clubhouse of the Royal Automobile Club is truly palatial would, therefore, be hackneyed. Let us just agree that the place is gargantuan and be done with it. Designed by Mewès and Davis – the architects behind the Ritz –the RAC has been called "the apotheosis of the West End Club". The foundations of the clubhouse had to be dug so deep that its builders unearthed seventeenth century cesspits, fossilised mammoth teeth, and a dinosaur's hip-bone. The building's façade is 228 feet long. Above the entrance four lofty pillars support a tympanum crowded with images declaring the triumph of the motor vehicle, such as a cherub riding a motorcycle.

The clubhouse boasts what an estate agent might term "impressive facilities". These include Turkish baths, an Italian marble swimming pool, squash courts, three restaurants, two bars, and a small private post office. Its food is undoubtedly the best in Clubland. Sadly the club's ten-pin bowling alley was discontinued in 1946, and its shooting range went (presumably with a bang) a little while later. In spite of these losses members are only rarely spotted loitering dejectedly on street corners.

In case they start to feel cramped in their London headquarters, members can always motor themselves over to Woodcote Park in Surrey, where the air is a little fresher, and another substantial clubhouse awaits them on land where once stood a twelfth century abbey.[17] Today a temple of motoring occupies this sacred site, which I suppose is evidence of what they call secularisation. An eighteenth century barn has been converted into a garage, in which the RAC maintains a fleet of historic motor vehicles.

The star of this collection is the Simms Motor Car, believed to be a prototype designed by the club's sainted founder. Although no documentary evidence exists to confirm its exact age, it is supposed that the Simms was constructed before 1900. A catalogue published by the RAC declares that the vehicle is "primitive", which seems a tad dismissive. Much better to think of it as prelapsarian; innocently unconcerned by the need for speed which soon

---

[17] Perhaps we might say that it is truly abbatial.

overtook motor manufacturing, and – how much worse – the desire for economy and efficiency in motors of our own day. With the original engine long since discarded, the car has been fitted with a later Simms stationary engine of 1902 construction, and is capable of achieving fifteen miles per hour on the open road. Hold onto your hats, chaps!

The car is steered by a tiller, like a boat, and the catalogue tells us that "on steep hills the passenger is required to dismount and assist with manoeuvring the car due to the absence of a reverse gear", which all sounds a bit much. Despite these inconveniences, the Simms has participated in the world's oldest motoring event, the RAC London to Brighton Veteran Car Run; an annual drive commemorating the first Emancipation Run. They sure don't build 'em like that anymore.

Simms was one of those men who liked to keep busy. His work with the internal combustion engine bridged the European and American markets, making him wealthy and influential. His entry in the *Oxford Dictionary of National Biography* suggests that Simms' "principal legacy to the automotive world was in the field of components, especially magnetos", but much more fun is his work into the military application of the motor vehicle, which resulted in the brilliantly butch Motor War Car. Intended for the Second Boer War, the conflict was over by the time the War Car trundled off the assembly line in 1902, and this fearsome armoured vehicle never saw action on the field of battle. In addition to this work, and founding what became the Royal Automobile Club, Simms also coined the words "petrol" and "motorcar". All in all, that is not a bad legacy for someone in his line of work.

9

THE OXFORD AND CAMBRIDGE CLUB

SALVAGED MEMBERS LIST

The problem with any taxonomy of Clubland is that there are almost as many ways to categorise clubs as there are clubs themselves. One of my preferred approaches is to consider the proportion of floorspace given over respectively to bars and to bookshelves. At one end of the spectrum is the Savage Club – which is 100% bar – and Oxford's Frewen Club – the library of which consists of a paperback edition of the 1982 *Guinness Book of World Records* and a well-thumbed copy of yesterday's *Racing Post*. At the other end lies the Oxford and Cambridge Club, which has set aside almost an entire floor of its substantial Pall Mall clubhouse for its libraries, plural. These beautiful rooms are the club's chief joy and are well used by a predictably bookish membership. The more bibulous bibliophiles will be pleased to note that there is also a substantial bar, recently refurbished in an art nouveau direction, and a terrace which is heavenly on a summer's afternoon with a glass of something chilled.

The Oxford and Cambridge Club (O&CC) is the product of a series of amalgamations. In 1938 the New University Club (NUC) merged with the United University Club (UUC); the most venerable of the Oxbridge clubs.[18] Then in 1972 it was the turn of the UUC to join forces with the Oxford and Cambridge University Club (O&CUC) on Pall Mall. As one old member commented, these clubs were rather like different houses of the same public school, with a rivalry that was playful rather than actual. I mention this bit of history not only to get your pulses racing,

---

[18] The UUC clubhouse on Suffolk Street was described as having "a grave and venerable air like a Doctor of Divinity". Its principal treasure was a first edition of the Authorised Bible, known to some as the "He" Bible because of the error in the *Book of Ruth* 3.15, when the title character is misgendered in a passage which reads: "And He went into the city".

but also because it is pertinent information regarding our *objet intéressant*.

This is a List of Members of the NUC, sent to a new member upon his election to the club in 1922. The gentleman in question was clutching this document as he boarded the P&O ocean liner *Egypt* on the 19th May 1922, bound for India. A heavy fog descended as the ship proceeded through the English Channel. As the guests dressed for dinner they lamented the poor weather and their slow progress. But the ship's captain had good reason to be cautious, for he knew that in addition to its human cargo, the *Egypt* was carrying a quantity of gold sovereigns and gold and silver bullion valued at one million pounds. This was the property of the British Government, and was being transported secretly to India and the Far East.

The captain was right to be worried. During supper the ship's diners were jolted from their seats by a dull, heavy thud which sent tables and waiters flying. The *Egypt* had been rammed by a French freighter, blinded by the fog, and a huge hole had been ripped in the ship's stern. Despite a swift evacuation eighty-eight people perished, and the vast store of gold and silver disappeared into the Atlantic Ocean off the coast of Brittany.

Divers could not descend safely to the depths to which the *Egypt* had sunk, but given the value of the ship's cargo it was not long before salvage attempts began. In 1929, a successful descent was made using a new sort of metal diving suit devised in Germany. There followed three years of slow and expensive salvaging. It was not until 1932 – ten years after the ship had sunk – that the salvage operation was concluded. It is said that 14,929 sovereigns, seventeen gold bars and thirty silver ingots still lie unaccounted for on the ocean floor.

Along with the gold and silver, there were retrieved some personal items belonging to the ship's passengers. This included the letter bearing news of election to the NUC, and the list of the club's current members. These documents were delivered to the Foreign Office, and into the hands of the *bon viveur*, Coptologist, and librarian, Sir Stephen Gaselee. Gaselee was one of those remarkable characters whom one feels sorry never to have met. As an undergraduate at Christ's Cambridge the sybaritic Gaselee had founded a dining club called the Deipnosophists', named for an ancient Greek cookbook which translates into English as *The Banquet of the Learned*.[19] The members wore purple dinner jackets lined with lilac silk and drank vodka.

Gaselee sent the waterlogged documents back to the NUC as a soggy souvenir of this maritime misadventure, where they were framed and mounted with due reverence. Following the amalgamations noted above, the list and description of the circumstances behind their recovery were displayed subsequently in the UUC, and then in the O&CUC. Almost a century after it was first issued, the list now hangs in a first floor corridor of the O&CC, between the smoking room and one of its libraries. It is a curious relic of a club that no longer exists, issued to a man whose identity has been lost, and commemorating a disaster which few now remember.

---

[19] Or more prosaically as *Sophists at Dinner*.

10

THE CARLTON CLUB

PRIMROSE LEAGUE MEMORABILIA

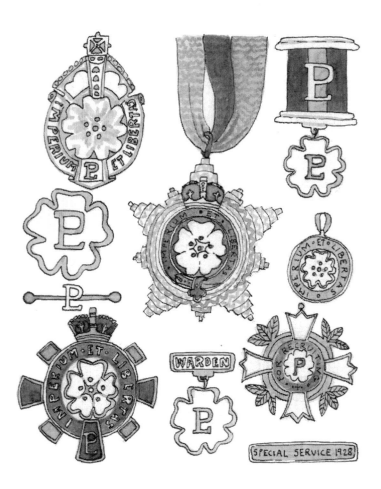

In retirement, the Duke of Wellington summarized the fruit of his life's learning: "Never write a letter to your mistress, and never join the Carlton Club." It is sad to note that few Conservative politicians have heeded this advice even in part. The Carlton was founded in 1832 to fight the Reform Bill, and spent the next century at the centre of English politics. In the first half of the twentieth century, the Carlton Club *was* the Conservative Party. Within its walls careers and cabinets were formed and obliterated. The Carlton's most famous political coup came in 1922 when Tory backbenchers met at the club to bring down David Lloyd George's coalition. When Ralph Blumenfeld, the American born editor of the *Daily Express*, was offered a knighthood for his supporting role in this drama, he declined and asked whether he might be granted membership of the Carlton instead. Such was the club's social cache at this time.

The Carlton has survived its fair share of upheaval. On 14th October 1940 the Luftwaffe dropped a bomb through its ceiling. Remarkably no one was hurt, although Viscount Soulbury later complained that "it took me nearly a fortnight to get the soot and grime out of my hair". The lack of fatalities led unkind voices in the Labour Party to comment that "the devil looks after his own". As a consequence of this bombing the Carlton relocated to its current, splendid, clubhouse on St James's; formerly the seat of Arthur's Club. Fifty years later the Carlton was hit by another bomb, this time planted by the IRA. Twenty were injured and Lord Kaberry later died from wounds sustained during the attack. The blast from the bomb was felt up to half a mile away.

Whilst the Carlton has never looked smarter than it does today, it is no longer a formidable political force. However, the subject of politics remains unavoidable. In 2018 it was not uncommon for members to be asked whether they would prefer "Brexit mustard" with their sausages, as opposed to the traitorous French variety.

The décor in the clubhouse is *réactionnaire chic*, leaning heavily on portraits of former Conservative grandees. Of all the men and women who have led the Tory Party, Benjamin Disraeli, the first (and last) Lord Beaconsfield is the most intriguing. Upon hearing of Disraeli's death in 1881 a young admirer mused in his dairy that, "No more curious figure ever appeared in English political life. He inspired affection, as well as admiration... He captivated the imagination of the English people, and triumphed over their not unnatural prejudices." Born into a Jewish family and laughed into submission at his first Common's speech, Disraeli's irrepressible wit, irresistible charm, and indefatigable self-belief helped him to overcome these impediments and to twice hold the highest political office in the land, whilst also finding time to write a series of successful, if to modern tastes turgid, novels.

Disraeli himself would rather have joined White's, and his pride was badly damaged when he was blackballed from that enclave of old Tory snobbishness. He was a regular fixture at the supper-table of Crockford's, along with fellow scribbler-cum-statesman, Edward Bulwer-Lytton. Disraeli was consequently a rather unenthusiastic member of the Carlton. After seeing off an attack by the hated Gladstone on the Second Reform Bill, jubilant members implored Disraeli to take his supper at the Carlton. The hero declined and headed home, where his wife greeted him with a pie from Fortnum and Mason's and a bottle of champagne. Disraeli responded with his famous quip, "Why, my dear, you are more like a mistress than a wife."[20]

---

[20] Gladstone was himself a member of the Carlton from 1833 until 1860, by which time he was Chancellor of the Exchequer in

It is typical of Lord Beaconsfield's decidedly camp approach to politics that his greatest legacy came in the form of a posthumous personality cult named for a wildflower. This was the Primrose League, founded in Disraeli's honour at the Carlton two years after his death, and commemorated in the club by a magnificent collection of badges, broaches, medals, ribbons, and banners.

The Primrose League was a political phenomenon like none before or since. It remains the largest mass membership organisation ever affiliated to a British political party, with over two million members at its peak. In the thirty years before the First World War it provided the Tories with an army of loyal activists, helping the party to triumph electorally in seats across Britain. The foundation of the League was a textbook piece of political opportunism. It was conducted by Lord Randolph Churchill (whose son, Winston, later addressed the League in glowing terms), and the soldier, spy, rake, and balloonist Frederick Gustavus Burnaby.[21] In the wake of Disraeli's death these men

---

Lord Palmerston's Liberal government. At this point it was suggested that if he did not resign, then he should be chucked out of the window in the direction of the Reform Club.
[21] See James Tissot's portrait of Burnaby in the uniform of the Household Cavalry.

sought to capitalise on the late leader's popularity by founding what amounted to a personality cult tied to a broad populist platform. The League was high on the sort of romantic, imperialistic rhetoric in which Disraeli had specialised, and correspondingly low on ideological intensity. Membership was open to all except "atheists and enemies of the British Empire", which ruled out far fewer persons than a contemporary Briton might imagine.

A significant part of the League's attraction was its magnificent regalia, inspired in equal parts by the Masons, the Orange Order, and the official Honours System. Tory grandees decided that "the Primrose League should be inferior to none of these in the variety of its regalia or the magniloquence of its titles." Working class men and women could style themselves as knights and dames of the League, and pin their medals to their Sunday best. Certain orders could be earned, such as service bars for successful electioneering, whilst others were purchased to raise money for the party. The most popular was the Jubilee Grand Star, instituted in 1887, which gives a good idea of the League's aesthetic. Its five points represented "the Empire in the five continents of the world". The Star was available in five designs for five different grades of membership, each complemented with a different ribbon.

The League was phenomenally popular. Men and women, servants and masters, Protestants and Catholics all rushed to join. Lord Lexden, in his history of the League, calls it "the most socially inclusive political organization the world had yet seen." The League was more than a political club, it was a lifestyle. Members could buy soap and coal, pens and parasols, all with the Primrose League stamp. The League had its own insurance scheme with generous pension coverage against sickness, old age, and death. Primrose Day – the anniversary of Disraeli's death on 19th April – saw vast celebrations across the nation. Children of the Primrose Buds marched through town squares singing:

Children of the Empire
Primrose Buds are we,
Marching, ever marching,
On to Victory,
Wearing still the emblem,
Just a tiny flower,
From our native woodlands,
Every joyful hour.

The humble primrose is not a flower that one necessarily associates with Disraeli. "The glorious lily, I think, was more to his taste", suggested Gladstone. Lady Knightly, the wife of a Tory backbencher, was less subtle, "I cannot stand the identification of the most simple and beautiful of flowers with one so artificial and stilted." Nevertheless, we have Disraeli's own word that he admired the primrose above all other blooms. Queen Victoria was besotted with Disraeli and would often send him bunches of flowers. After one such delivery, Disraeli wrote to his sovereign, "Of all the flowers, the one that retains its beauty longest [is the] sweet primrose, the ambassador of Spring." The flower was in bloom as Disraeli died, and the association stuck.

The League flourished in the late Victorian and Edwardian eras, but its influence was not to survive the First World War. With the franchise expanded to the entire adult population, politics had moved on, and the activities of the League soon became an irrelevance. Although the legacy of the Primrose League has been widely forgotten, the Carlton Club's collection of memorabilia bears sparkling witness to this colourful chapter in the history of the Conservative Party, a chapter authored within its own walls. "Church and Empire" may no longer be a rallying cry to inspire the British people, but if modern politicians should take anything from the story of the Primrose League, it is that one should never underestimate the appeal of high quality merchandise.

11

PRATT'S CLUB

STATUETTE OF THE BUDDHA

A friend once rented an attic room in Albany because he thought that the address would prove irresistible to the ladies. Up to a point, Lord Copper. One evening he brought home an Eastern European beauty whom he had met at a party in Mayfair. The hallowed address meant nothing to her, except that it was nearby. Entering from Savile Row her pretty brow began to cloud. Things did not improve when they began ascending the stairs to his garret. "Why", she enquired with a plaintive note in her voice, "do the English aristocracy choose to live in such squalor?" This sublime utterance was not intended as a witticism – I don't think the poor girl had any wits about her – it was an earnest question. The sheiks and oligarchs of the oil rich nations would not be caught dead in Albany. Perhaps it is this restrained tendency that has enabled the English aristocracy to survive so long with their necks intact.

Around the corner from Albany there is another example of aristocratic understatement: Pratt's Club. One must travel to other corners of Clubland in search of Edwardian opulence, acres of libraries, squash courts, or – Heaven help us – a business suite. Pratt's is conducted on an altogether more modest scale.

The club's unflattering moniker is not a comment on the intellectual vitality of the membership, but rather a tribute to William Nathanial Pratt, formerly croupier at Crockford's and steward to the 7th Duke of Beaufort. One evening in 1841, Beaufort, wearied by his usual high-society hijinks, decided to drop round to Pratt's house with a few chums. It was the mid-Victorian equivalent of "a quiet night in with the lads". The evening was passed drinking and gaming in Pratt's cosy little basement. Beaufort enjoyed himself so much that he began to make a habit of stopping by, and in time these informal wassails ossified into Pratt's Club.

Although smarter rooms were soon made available, the duke's party preferred to stay downstairs in the kitchen. And here, like moles or radishes or other agreeable things that live underground, the members of Pratt's remain. In terms of décor, this subterranean lair represents a full-blooded riposte to the principals of *feng shui*; its unstudied clutter conjuring the ambience of some ancient country pub. As far as amenities go, there is a billiards room, but as billiards is not much played this room functions principally as a place to discard coats and umbrellas.

Anthony Sampson described Pratt's as being full "of stuffed fishes, birds, bric-a-brac, and surprising members". Pratt's was Harold Macmillan's favourite club (he belonged to six), and Winston Churchill once cooked a meal personally on the kitchen range after a late sitting at Parliament. Pratt's high conservatism is best illustrated by the blackballing of the Old Etonian Tory MP David Price "because he abstained at Suez and opposed the death penalty."

As to the fishes and birds, Pratt's Club is probably where wicked vegans go when they die. It is stuffed with stuffed critters. Aside from the quotidian fowls and fish there is the head of a rhinoceros, which lies prone on the dining room floor. It has been suggested that this monumental work of the taxidermist's art has only ever been seen by two women. The first is the club's female servant, called Georgina, which is not her real name, but follows the convention that all members of staff are known as George. The other is Her Majesty the Queen, who was invited down by the 11th Duke of Devonshire, then the owner of Pratt's. She is said to have remarked, "what a large rhinoceros for such a small room."[22] Hidden behind a velvet curtain

---

[22] There used to be a tradition, I do not know if it still holds, that no woman could even telephone Pratt's. If a wife attempted to

are the jaws of a hippopotamus and a duck-billed platypus.

Among the hunting prints, silver jugs, rugs, clocks, antlers, oodles of taxidermy, and dresser full of old china there are a few items which deserve closer attention. Pratt's chimney piece panels appear to have been lifted from a country house. Each contains a classical frieze, which the 11th Duke of Devonshire used to claim were executed by Praxiteles. I am not sure whether the 12th Duke – the current owner – maintains the same pretence. Then there are a couple of pieces from the Orient, which seem out of place in so resolutely Occidental a setting: a Tibetan prayer wheel and a small statuette of the Buddha. This little devotional statue sits in a niche above a seldom-used cribbage table. It was presented to Pratt's by Lord Frederic Spencer Hamilton, author of the incomparably titled memoir, *The Vanished Pomps of Yesterday*.[23]

Hamilton was a typical Pratt's man: Tory MP, younger son of a duke, sportsman (he claimed the credit for

---

reach her husband then one of the Georges would respond, "Madam, no married member is ever in the club."

[23] Also *Here, There and Everywhere*, and *The Days Before Yesterday*.

having brought skiing to Canada), literary dabbler, bachelor, and traveller. As a diplomat, Hamilton spent time stationed in Canada, Russia, South America, and across the Far East. He was, in the parlance of our own age, a man with a good work/life balance, which is to say that he viewed the diplomatic service principally as a means to hunt new animals and to woo new duchesses.

A case in point. In 1881 Hamilton was based in St Petersburg when Tsar Alexander II was assassinated. For the next six months, all civil liberties were curtailed and police repression was violent and widespread. Hamilton does not note any of this in *The Vanished Pomps of Yesterday*, but he does lament the termination of court life during this time of national mourning. With no balls to attend, Hamilton decamped to the Gulf of Finland where he spent a very jolly time shooting wolves, fishing, and tobogganing. "It will be seen that in one way or another", he concludes after ten pages of this, "there was no lack of amusement to be found around Petrograd, even during the entire cessation of Court and social entertainments". *The Vanished Pomps of Yesterday* was first published in 1920, and offers absolutely no insights into the seething discontent which led to the Russian Revolution three years previously.

Back to the statuette of the Buddha. Baron Ormathwaite, who owned Pratt's from 1907 until 1937, used to pester Hamilton to fetch him some token of the Orient which might be displayed in the clubhouse. The old diplomat complied by heading East, well three miles North-East actually, to Islington. He bought this statue in the market on the Caledonian Road and presented it to Pratt's. In true Clubland style, this unremarkable object is still there a century later. Another bit of bric-a-brac in need of dusting, another story to be told.

12

BROOKS'S CLUB

NAPOLEON'S DEATH MASK

Brooks's is one of three surviving Regency era clubs on St James's Street. This cluster of discreet mansions is the omphalos of Clubland. A wag once said that Brooks's Club resembles "a Duke's house – with the Duke lying dead upstairs", but really it has never been a sleepy club. In its early years the behaviour of its

members could barely even be considered civilised, at least by later standards. Gambling was the principal reason that a Regency clubman came to St James's, and huge fortunes were acquired and disbursed on the gaming tables of Brooks's and White's.

Charles James Fox was a man prone to excess in all earthly pleasures except dress (he took to wearing the blue jacket and buff waistcoat which had been the uniform of George Washington's armies). Immoderation was instilled in the young Charles by his father, who encouraged his son to drink and womanize whilst he was still at Eton. Elected to membership of Brooks's at the age of only sixteen, Fox spent the rest of his life in and out of Clubland. He once played dice at Brooks's from a Tuesday evening until 5 p.m. the following afternoon. Having initially gained £12,000, he ended down £11,000; and this at a time when money was money. As one account of this binge reported: "The following day he made what was, not surprisingly, a lamentable speech in the House of Commons on the 39 Articles, dined in Brooks's at 11.30 p.m., went onto White's where he drank until 7 a.m., thence to Almack's where he won £6,000 before setting out for Newmarket races next day at 4 p.m." Truly there were giants in the earth in those days. It is a popular myth that the gaming table at Brooks's has a semi-circular space cut out of one side to accommodate Fox's prodigious girth; actually it is for the croupier, but let us not have a little fact get in the way of a good story.[24]

This gambling took place in the Great Subscription Room. Its walls were bare so as not to distract the men from their cards. Now it houses two large canvasses of the Dilettanti Society, painted by Sir Joshua Reynolds. Horace Walpole dismissed the Dilettanti as "a club, for which the nominal qualification is having been in Italy, and the real one, being drunk: the two chiefs are Lord Middlesex and Sir Francis Dashwood, who were seldom sober the whole time they were in Italy." These pictures embody the motto of the Dilettanti: *Seria Ludo* (roughly, serious subjects approached in a light-hearted manner). The first painting shows the collector Sir William Hamilton surrounded by seven of his fellow Dilettanti, pointing to an engraving of a Greek vase. In the second picture, seven more Dilettanti examine a collection of antique gems. In both paintings wine is flowing, knowing looks are being exchanged, and ribald gestures are being made.

---

[24] Fox cast a long (as well as a broad) shadow over Brooks's. When the club was split into factions following Gladstone's Home Rule Bill, the ghost of Charles James Fox was reportedly seen haunting the corridors. More sceptical members said that it was probably just a fat servant carrying a bottle of port.

A lady's garter is being toasted, a sex act is being intimated. *Seria Ludo* indeed.

The Dilettanti have also made their mark in the library, a late nineteenth century addition to the clubhouse. Here hang the twenty-three portraits of the Dilettanti painted by George Knapton between 1741 and 1749, when the society was at the height of its lunacy. Most of the members are pictured in costume. Dashwood, gazing lustily at the pudenda of the Medici Venus, appears as a Franciscan monk, a reference to the bacchanalian and blasphemous "Hellfire Club" over which he presided at Medmenham Abbey.[25]

It is a testimony to Brooks's curatorial excellence that these magnificent portraits are not even the most arresting feature of the library. This honour belongs to a mounted bronze death mask of the Emperor Napoleon, a morbid object caught up in an unfolding historical debate.

In the days before photography, it was common practice to make plaster or wax casts of notable

---

[25] This behaviour appears all the more scandalous when one remembers that Dashwood was Chancellor of the Exchequer from 1762 to 1763.

persons' faces immediately following their death. When Napoleon died on St Helena in May 1821 he was the most famous man in Europe, and within days of the Emperor's death different versions of his death mask began circulating.[26] Who made the first mask is still a matter of disagreement. Some maintain that it was Napoleon's personal physician, Francois Carlo Antommarchi. Other records suggest that it was Francis Burton, a British Army surgeon who presided at the Emperor's autopsy, and who cast the original mould during the post-mortem. If this is the case then Antommarchi, who waited until Burton's death to commercialise his mask, stole his imprint from the British surgeon's original. The plot is further complicated by rumours that Madame Bertrand, Napoleon's attendant on St Helena, stole part of Burton's original cast, leaving the surgeon with only the ears and the back of the head. According to this theory, Bertrand was sued unsuccessfully by Burton for custody of the mask. The following year, Madame Bertrand gave this mask to Antommarchi, from which

---

[26] Madame Tussaud made a wax model of Napoleon on his deathbed which became a favourite exhibition in her touring show. In 1835 her museum found a permanent home on Baker Street. A regular visitor was the Duke of Wellington, who would stand by the exhibit for long stretches, gazing down at his vanquished foe. When Wellington died he was also immortalised in wax, and placed beside his former rival, standing looking down at the waxwork Napoleon as he had done in life.

he created several copies. One of these was sent to the renowned sculptor Antonio Canova, but Canova died before he was able to produce a sculpture using the mask.

Whoever took the original imprint, copies of these death masks cast in bronze and marble were soon seen in the markets of Europe. Napoleon's body had begun to decompose in the fierce heat of St Helena and, as was noted at the time, his features had changed markedly. The final image we have of Napoleon is therefore softer than the portraits painted during his lifetime.

Quite how this death mask came to Brooks's we do not know. Like so many of Clubland's treasures, its origins have been lost to history. But Brooks's decision to display this relic of the Corsican Fiend is down to no mere whim. For its first century, the club was a hotbed of Whiggery. In Viscount Melbourne's short-lived Whig cabinet of 1834 every single minister was a member of Brooks's. The construction of the Reform Club in 1836 shifted the bastion of liberal politics in Clubland from St James to Pall Mall, but as late as 1905 twelve out of twenty-five members of Sir Henry

Campbell-Bannerman's Liberal cabinet were also members of Brooks's.

Napoleon's rise to power had widespread support in Brooks's, and some members followed his later career with something approaching pride. Brooks's dalliance with Napoleonism reached a head in 1815. In June of that year, Lord Grey and Sir Robert Wilson announced to a packed clubhouse the inevitability of Napoleon's victory at Waterloo. The two statesmen were just explaining how the Emperor was at that moment taking possession of Brussels when a clamour on the street below drew members to the window. From here they could view a great victory parade which was making its way down St James's, headed by the captured *Aigle de drapeau*. Seen in this context the death mask appears as both a shrine to a lost cause, and an admirably self-aware gesture of magnanimity in defeat.

13

BOODLE'S CLUB

CARTOON OF SIR FRANK STANDISH BY JAMES GILLRAY

A Standing-dish at Boodles.

In episode seven of his peerless television series *Civilisation*, Kenneth Clark stands in the Vatican's Gallery of Maps and wonders aloud "if a single thought that has helped forward the human spirit has ever been conceived or written down in an enormous room." Clark turns to leave, and the camera pans out slowly to reveal the full vastness of the gallery as the closing music plays. A late flourishing of a particularly patrician genus of anti-Catholicism, it is one the great moments in the history of television. Clark's point is a good one. Overly large rooms are built to intimidate or to impress, to bludgeon their visitors into an attitude of submission; they are not built with a view to human habitation. The clubs of Britain are mercifully short on enormous rooms. The dining room of the National Liberal was once vast, before they chopped it in half to create a bar. Predictably, one must cross the Atlantic to find BIG clubs with BIG rooms. Take the Union League Club of Chicago. It covers twenty-three floors, each one of which contains a ballroom or library in which one could fit several smaller clubs, and possibly some of the smaller European states.

No. 28 St James's Street, by contrast, is built on a human scale, and this is the source of its timeless charm. It is not quite the smartest clubhouse in London, though it comes close. This is the only building in the capital attributed to John Crunden, who designed it in 1775 for the sybaritic *Savoir Vivre* Club. Boodle's moved in eight years later and no-one has persuaded them to move out since. The grandest room is the saloon, which is a perfect example of domestic Adamesque. Despite its high ceiling, magnificent chandelier, and rich decoration, the saloon is not an enormous room in the Clarkian sense. It is perfectly conducive to thinking thoughts which might conceivably help forward the human spirit.

In its early days Boodle's did have a few thinkers; among them Adam Smith, David Hume, and Edward "Scribble, Scribble, Scribble" Gibbon. But it has never been what one might call a thinking-man's club (it has no library to speak of). The second oldest club in London (after White's), Boodles was founded in 1762 by *habitués* of Almack's on Pall Mall. It was named for its head waiter, Edwin Boodle, an *émigré* from Oswestry. Boodle's began as a political club, for friends of Lord Shelburne. It was probably with Boodle's in mind that Dr Johnson wrote of Shelburne, "I don't say he is a man I would set at the head of a nation, though perhaps he may be as good as the next Prime Minister that comes, but he is a man to be at the head of a club." Whereas Brooks's and White's continued to flex their political muscles into the twentieth century, Boodle's political aspirations evaporated soon after moving to No. 28 St James's. Perhaps this is part of the reason that Boodle's is not spoken of in the same hushed tone reserved for Brooks's and White's. As Lejeune comments, "the remarkable thing about the club's 200 years of history is how uneventful they seem to have been." The subsequent fifty years have been no different. It was for other clubs to provoke, to ferment, to sparkle with brilliance. Boodle's became a club for country gentlemen. It has close ties to the county of Shropshire, and the membership has long been caricatured as a collection of "Sir Johns" more interested in farming than in fashion.

The item which best captures the spirit of the club is a hand-coloured cartoon by James Gillray, published in May 1800. It depicts Sir Frank Standish, a Lancastrian Baronet, sitting idly at the window of Boodle's. His arms are folded, his rounded belly bulges through his breeches, and his riding hat is jammed squarely on his head.[27] He is the very model of a stolid country squire. An unremarkable man, the Standish Baronetcy

---

[27] A short digression on the wearing of hats in clubs. Every polite boy knows not to wear his hat indoors. Yet it was not always so in Clubland. In some clubs, right up to the middle of the nineteenth century, hats were worn at all times. At the Oxford and Cambridge Club members retained their hats whilst dining, as a statement that they were as comfortable in their club as in their own homes. In others, such as the Garrick, hats were removed and stored under one's chair during mealtimes, and placed on the chimneypiece in the library when dozing. The matter could be contentious. One member of the Oriental, forbidden to wear his hat when dining, vowed never to eat at that club again.

became extinct upon Sir Frank's death. He was, it seems, more interested in horses than in women (fillies rather than *fillies*).

Why did Britain's greatest political cartoonist choose to satirise this provincial mediocrity? From 1797 until his death in 1815, Gillray lived and worked above the print shop of Hannah Humphrey, located at no. 27 St James's: next door to Boodle's. The preposterous figure of Sir Frank Standish, framed by Boodle's bow window, must have been a constant companion and the urge to mock proved irresistible. Gillray's cartoon is titled "A Standing-dish at Boodles", a pun on a "standing dish" – a dish seen every day. The subtitle "Vide: a d___d good Cocoa-Tree pun" refers to the Cocoa Tree, a contemporary club which occupied no. 64 St James's. On the wall behind Standish, Gillray has included a picture of a horse, captioned "Yellow Filly". Here as always, Gillray was bang on the mark. Boodle's men tend to be hippophiles and this is reflected in the club's choice of art. A series of Grand National winners, owned by the same member, hang on the staircase.

Gillray's cartoon has two further significances. First, it is an early example of the club cartoon, a genre so popular that no club lavatory is without its own example. Cartoonists are attracted to clubs because they provide an unparalleled opportunity for social observation. Stuffy retired majors, clueless guests, the collective horror of womenfolk; it is a rich comic seam with plenty of material left to mine.

Secondly, Sir Frank Standish sits at Boodle's bow window. This is one of a pair of famous bow windows looking out on St James's. The other is the so-called Beau Window at White's, once occupied by Beau Brummell and his cronies. Sir Winston Churchill was made an honorary member of Boodle's after the Second World War, an honour usually reserved for royalty. When he visited the club with Harold Macmillan and Lord Cherwell he announced that it had long been an ambition of his to sit in the bow window and smoke a cigar. He did so, to the delight of the crowd which gathered beneath. I prefer the story of the cantankerous old duke who always staked out his spot at the window on dreary days. Why? Because he enjoyed "watching the damned people get wet". What was I saying about Boodle's being a conducive setting for thoughts to forward the human spirit...?

14

WHITE'S CLUB

BETTING BOOK

White's is to Clubland what the Vatican is to Catholicism. Perhaps this is a clumsy analogy because these days they let anyone into the Vatican, even Jesuits. Every clubman is inclined to think his club superior, but for members of White's this is a matter of fact and not mere bluster. As Anthony Lejeune wrote in his tricentennial history of the club: "The fact remains that all other London clubs – one is tempted to say all the other clubs in the world – have generally and generously been prepared to acknowledge that White's is special." This attitude derives in part from White's seniority. White's is the Ur-Club. It is a year older than the Bank of England, and was founded when there was still a Stuart on the throne.

Every prime minister from Walpole to Peel was a member, and although never narrowly party-political, White's has usually been cast as the conservative counterpart to Brooks's. As late as 1964 Anthony Sampson could write that "the most gruesome assembly of old Tories remains White's... with its proud tradition of philistinism". Alas, these are less clubbable times. David Cameron resigned his membership of White's over the inevitable issue of wimmin accompanied by a fanfare of self-righteous toots; this despite his father having been the club's chairman.

During the Regency period, White's stolid Tory fare was leavened by an outbreak of dandyism. It was from White's famous bow window – dubbed "that sacred semi-circle" by Sir William Fraser – that Beau

Brummell dissected the fashion choices of those lesser mortals on the street below. More than High Toryism, high fashion, high camp, or high anything else, White's is best known for high stakes gambling. In 1756 Horace Walpole and some of his chums produced a piece of heraldic satire for the club, a bas-relief version of which may be found in the front hall. Walpole described its symbolism thus:

> The blazon is vert (for a card-table); three parolis proper on a chevron sable (for a Hazard table); two rouleaux in saltire between two dice proper, on a canton sable; a white ball (for election) argent. The supporters are an old and young knave of clubs; the crest, an arm out of an earl's coronet shaking a dice-box; and the motto, *Cogit amor nummi* – "The love of money compels." Round the arms is a claret-bottle ticket by way of order.

To witness the full scale of White's wagering, one needs to consult the club's infamous Betting Book, volumes of which date back to 1743. (The original book was destroyed by fire in 1733. The firemen tackling the blaze received personal encouragement from King

George II and the Prince of Wales, who were on hand within the hour. Alas, to no avail).[28] Betting books used to be commonplace. From Oxbridge common rooms to suburban golf clubs, they provided a light-hearted outlet for competitive temperaments. The Betting Book of White's is conducted on an altogether grander scale than such provincial penny-pushing.

The first entry, written in a faded copperplate, is dated "Octr. ye 5, 1743": "Ld Lincoln bets Ld Winchilsea One hundred guineas to fifty guineas, that the Duchess Dowager of Marlborough does not survive the Duchess Dowager of Cleveland". A few pages later the elegant copperplate – presumably the work of the proprietor or some member of his staff – gives way to a multiplicity of scrawls. Some wag has written on this page, "About this time it is supposed that the nobility of England began to learn to write."

In the club's Georgian heyday, the Betting Book was notable both for the vastness and for the inventiveness of the wagers. The aristocracy were far richer in the mid-eighteenth century than they had been a

---

[28] The fire features in Hogarth's *A Rake's Progress*. The gamblers do not notice the conflagration, so consumed are they by their dice and cards.

generation previously, and they had access to generous credit from a growing number of established banks. (One noble family after the Second World War was still paying off a mortgage first contracted in the 1790s.) Flush with cash, the members of White's bet on anything and everything: on births and deaths; on horses and divorces; on battles and hangings; on the strength of earthquakes and the pronunciation of French nouns; even on one famous occasion on which of two raindrops would be the first to reach the windowsill, with £3000 (in 1816) at stake. It has been said of White's membership that:

> They were not religious, but had any member become clairvoyant and announced the imminent sounding of the Last Trump, a book at once would have been opened on the event, with side-bets taken on which of the arch-angels would be the one to sound it.

Some of the bets were downright immoral. Walpole told a story – probably untrue – of a man who fell ill outside the club. The members immediately began to take bets on whether he was alive or dead. When it was proposed that the man's blood be taken, those who had betted on his being dead objected, arguing that this would prejudice the fairness of the wager. Walpole told another, even more disturbing tale. "One of the youths at White's", he recorded, "betted £1000 that a man could live twelve hours under water. He hired a desperate fellow, sunk him in a ship by way of experiment and both ship and man have not appeared since."

The star of the Betting Book during gambling's golden era was William Douglas, the Earl of March and Ruglen, better known by his later title, the 4th Duke of Queensberry, and better still as "Old Q". Old Q was thoroughly disreputable old bachelor. "In the balcony of no. 138, Piccadilly, on fine days in summer," wrote Leigh Hunt, "used to sit this withered old figure, with one eye looking on all the females that passed him, and not displeased if they returned him whole winks for a single one. This was the Most Noble William Douglas, Duke, Marquess, and Earl of Queensbury."

Douglas' bets are the stuff of legend. One of the most famous concerned a "chaise match", when Count Taaffe wagered Old Q that he could not provide a four-wheeled carriage, drawn by four horses and carrying a man, that could cover nineteen miles in a single hour.

Douglas diverted all his considerable resources towards winning the bet. He auditioned horse after horse, sought out the slightest possible driver, and commissioned an entirely new sort of carriage made of lightweight wood and whalebone. The course was run in 53 minutes and 27 seconds, much to the delight of the crowds who flocked to witness this spectacle on Newmarket Heath. A print of the bizarre vehicle is retained by White's in memory of this bet.

On another occasion, Old Q boasted that he could cause a letter to be delivered to a destination fifty miles away in a single hour; a feat which would test the Royal Mail today. The bet was taken eagerly by several members, but these persons did not count on Old Q's legendary cunning, and failed to specify the mode of delivery. This was to be their downfall. The wily peer stuffed the letter inside a cricket ball, which was relayed over the course of fifty miles by a chain of sportsmen, throwing the ball one to another. In such a manner the distance was covered with time to spare.

By the nineteenth century, the quality of wagers at White's had stagnated; they became neither so ambitious nor so ruinous. One commentator has characterised the members of this period as "chiefly

115

occupied with two subjects, the comparative longevity of their male friends and the fertility of their female ones." There are some playful exceptions. In 1825: "Lord Binning bets Lord Falmouth five guineas that a Roman Catholic Bishop upon formally abjuring his Catholic faith, may be made a Protestant Bishop without any new ordination in the Protestant Church." In 1856: "Mr F. Cavendish bets Mr H. Brownrigg 2/1 that he does not kill the bluebottle fly before he goes to bed." (Mr Brownrigg dispatched his quarry and won the 2/1.)

As a rule, the landed aristocracy of our own day have neither the outlandish inclinations nor the abundant resources of their forefathers. White's is therefore less boisterous, less risqué, less dissolute than once it was. Nevertheless, as one clubman has enthused, at White's "there remains a touch of aristocratic raffishness which has vanished from the rest of Clubland". Time, like an ever rolling wotsit, might bear all its thingies away, but White's remains Clubland's Holy of Holies.

15

THE CAVALRY AND GUARDS CLUB

PICTURE OF VALENTINE BAKER AND EDWARD VII

Since its foundation in 1810 the Guards Club was essentially peripatetic, occupying properties around St James's before finally making camp at No. 70 Pall Mall. Here the Guardsmen commissioned the first clubhouse to be built on what is now the world's most magnificent parade of clubs; where the army leads, the rest follow. By the 1970s the club was struggling financially, and in '75 the Guardsmen upped-sticks once again, this time to join forces with the Cavalry Club on Piccadilly. The Guardsmen brought with them a number of *objets d'art* as well as enough members to bolster the cash-strapped Cavalry Club. The two clubs were already united by a shared sense of social distinction. It was not until the 1970s that the Guards Club admitted officers of the Welsh and Irish Guards, whilst an account of the Cavalry Club from 1963 noted wryly that just because the cavalry regiments were now all mechanized, this did not mean that officers of the Royal Tank Regiment were welcome to join.

Thus in 1976 a new club was born at a time when many similar establishments were closing their doors for good. The result of this happy union is an amply stocked clubhouse. There are trophies for polo and pig-sticking, captured enemy ensigns, an Elizabethan leather shoe found in the attic of a former Guards clubhouse, a ceremonial stick presented by Oliver Cromwell to the victor of Stockport Bridge, and an unexpected portrait of Kaiser Wilhelm II wearing a very silly avian helmet. In the hallway, regimental drums have been repurposed as lampstands, whilst the coffee room is jollified by an extensive collage of *Vanity Fair* caricatures.

Amongst the more notable paintings is a large equine scene featuring Edward VII when Prince of Wales, with his good friend Valentine Baker. Stylistically, the painting is unremarkable. Attributed to Sir Francis Grant, it shows the two men reviewing the 10th Royal Hussars at Aldershot in 1871. The interest lies with the relationship between Bertie and Baker, and how this was tested three years after this scene was painted.

Valentine Baker was a rising star of the British cavalry; handsome, heroic, and beloved by his men. He distinguished himself in the 1850s as a gallant young officer in South Africa, and was lauded as an innovator and a brilliant military strategist. Promotion to the rank of colonel in the fashionable 10th Royal Hussars came at the age of only 33. It should perhaps be noted that this rank was attained before Cardwell's abolition of purchase, so Baker's money counted as much as his talents in procuring this position.[29] It was in the 10th that Baker developed a great friendship with the Prince of Wales, the regiment's colonel-in-chief.

---

[29] William III, Queen Anne, and George I had all tried to abolish purchase but were unsuccessful. It survived only because of the parsimony of Parliament, which would have had to find money to fill the gap once this obvious anachronism was removed.

In 1874, Baker was appointed assistant quartermaster-general at Aldershot, a role which was supposed to guarantee his promotion to the rank of general. Instead an incident took place on a train which scandalised the nation. In a case which shows that there is nothing new under the sun, the rakish cavalry officer was accused by a young woman of having made unwanted sexual advances. Trains in those days did not have corridors, so when Baker entered the carriage occupied by Miss Rebecca Dickinson, she had no easy way of avoiding his wandering hands. Miss Dickinson was sufficiently distressed to open the door whilst the train was speeding between Woking and Esher, climbing down onto the running-board in order to escape the colonel. When the case was heard three months later, Baker was found guilty of indecent assault and sentenced to a year's imprisonment. "He will be disgraced for life!" wrote Queen Victoria. "What is to happen if officers, high in position, behave as none of the lowest would have dared to, unless a severe example is made? I own I feel most indignant."

Baker was not disgraced for life, however. He experienced a very Victorian rehabilitation. After Baker's release the Prince of Wales arranged for his friend to serve with the Turkish army, where once again Baker proved his talent for warfare in the Russo-Turkish War of 1877. "I swear by the Prophet", wrote one Turkish officer, "that the Infidel who commands our cavalry fights with the courage of ten thousand tigers." The cavalryman gained the nickname "Baker Pasha" and his exploits became regular tabloid fodder back in Blighty.

The Prince of Wales tried repeatedly to have his friend reinstated in the British Army. In 1887 the Queen at last relented, but Baker died of fever on the banks of the Nile before news of his pardon arrived. He was accorded a funeral with full British military rights. It has been suggested that one indirect consequence of the Baker Affair was the later introduction of corridors onto trains. The Cavalry Club was founded three years after Baker's death, becoming a popular haunt of the future monarch who refused to abandon his troublesome friend.

16

THE CALEDONIAN CLUB

RAM'S HEAD SNUFF MULL

It used to be thought that Clubland was the invention of a Scotsman. William Macall, the story went, started his career as valet to the Duke of Hamilton, the senior duke in the Scottish Peerage. On leaving Hamilton's service, Macall made his way to London's St James's district and changed his name to Almack to counter any anti-Scottish prejudice. The coffee house and gambling den which Almack founded evolved into

Boodle's and Brooks's. Actually, this story is only true in part. Almack seems to have come from Thirsk in North Yorkshire, not Scotland, and his name was never Macall. The Scottish rumour was spread in Almack's own lifetime, so it is at least as old as Clubland itself. But we have to wait until the late nineteenth century to find a distinctively Scottish presence in London's Clubland.

The Caledonian Club is housed in an elegant neo-Georgian mansion in Belgravia, a wee dauner from the heart of Clubland. As the name suggests, it is a club for Scots and Scot-lovers, and the clubhouse is festooned with memories of the Auld Country. There is a shrine to Rabbie Burns in the hallway; MacNabs and MacGregors with muckle hairy sporrans strike Romantic poses within their mezzotints; and the bar is stocked with enough whisky to see the entire cast of *Trainspotting* though the winter. The club has some fine oil paintings of the Scottish Highlands, which make one long to walk through that sublime, prehistoric landscape. In its spirit, the Caledonian seems to group together with the service clubs; like the Cavalry and Guards or the Rag, members of the Caledonian can share the sense of being sojourners in London, with their hearts belonging elsewhere.

In 1940 a Luftwaffe bomb blasted open the Caledonian's former home in St James's, destroying much of the interior. One object which survived the attack was a ram's head snuff mull, donated in 1923 by then chairman J.A. Milne. "Mull" is Scottish dialect for mill, referring to the grinding of tobacco. There was something of a craze for ram's head snuff mulls in Victorian and Edwardian Scotland, particularly in regiments wishing to preserve something of a beloved ovine mascot. The mull in the possession of the Caledonian is not even the only one in Clubland; there is another fine example in the Oriental, formerly the property of the Byculla Club of Bombay.

The head is a gruesome hairy thing, framed by spectacular curly horns tipped with citrine set thistles. Sitting upon the beast's head like a sultan's turban or a Russian onion dome, is the silver snuff receptacle. This too is embossed with thistles. Dangling down over the ram's glossy eyes are four small tools, each attached to a silver chain. There is a little rake and a pricker to smooth out lumps, a miniature spoon to scoop out the good stuff, and a tiny duster for cleaning the snuff-taker's moustaches. The overall effect is of course absurd. No wonder the ram in all its silver finery appears to be smirking. Tragically, if bathetically, the snuff mull also functions as a war memorial. Milne gave the thing in memory of his son, Captain Johnnie Milne of the Royal Flying Corps, who was shot down over Flanders in May 1917. A plaque inserted between the eyes reports the details.

The practice of taking snuff became popular in England towards the end of the seventeenth century. It was known a little earlier in France and first arrived in Britain through Scotland, because of that country's diplomatic ties to the French court. The tobacco lords of Glasgow became the major importers, and the sign used to denote a shop selling snuff was that of a Scottish Highlander in full fig. As the habit gained popularity, paraphernalia associated with snuff-taking became increasingly elaborate. Never one to do things by halves, Lord Byron once spent five hundred guineas on "seven gold snuff boxes" and "seven snuff boxes of gold and silver gilt" in a single shopping trip. In addition to its snuff mull, the Caledonian also possesses an elaborately carved rootwood snuff box, depicting scenes from Rabbie Burns' ghoulish epic *Tam o' Shanter*.

Snuff maintained its popularity deep into the nineteenth century. Charles Darwin, an inveterate snuff-taker whose moustache was stained brown from the habit, once stuck some snuff up a monkey's nose to study its emotions. "It closed its eyelids whilst sneezing", recorded the father of evolutionary science, "but not on a subsequent occasion whilst uttering loud cries".

By the dawn of the twentieth century, snuff was no longer the cultural force that it had once been. It had become a habit for poor people with poor taste, dismissed by Laurie Lee as the "Reeking substance of the under-world, clay-brown dust of decay, of powdered flesh and crushed old bones, rust-scrapings, and the rubbish of graves". "Some few clubs still retain the snuff-box which once featured on the mantelpiece of every club", records a history of 1911. "In most, however, it has disappeared. Snuff-taking has become obsolete since the triumph of the cigarette – perhaps a more pernicious habit." How true. Today, like so much that is good, the habit is confined to Clubland and a few other citadels of reaction. Yet with the smoking ban in full force across Britain, perhaps we are living on the cusp of a new dawn for the Scottish snuff industry. Not an idea to be sniffed at.

17

THE ROYAL THAMES YACHT CLUB

BONE MODEL OF THE *ROYAL GEORGE*

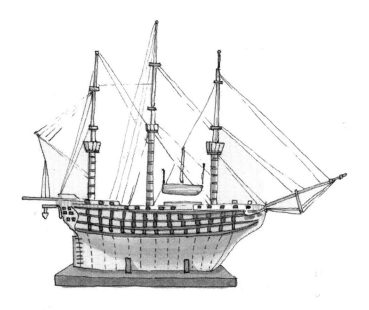

I'm a generous fellow and this book takes a capacious approach to Clubland, but there are species of club which do not come within its purview. The working men's club is a commendable breed of club, but it is not *our* sort of club. The golf club, the tennis club, and the tiddlywinks club are all valid forms of club, but they are not *our* clubs. Likewise, the yacht club lies outside the scope of this digressive but landlocked volume. All that is except the Royal Thames Yacht Club. For one thing, the Royal Thames has a coffee room in which one does not take coffee, an indication of the club's pedigree, and a sure sign that it belongs in Clubland. It also has a quarterdeck and refers to its bedrooms as cabins, which would be eccentric in any of our other clubs (apart, perhaps, from the Eccentric). It is therefore a sort of hybrid species.

"The Thames", as the club is known to its members, is Europe's oldest continuously operating yacht club, established in 1775 when the country's yacht racing took place on a rather wider River Thames. The club was originally christened "the Cumberland Fleet", after its founder, the Duke of Cumberland and met at first in a succession of coffee houses. From 1857, the Thames leased or owned properties in the West End, before purchasing Hyde Park House, Knightsbridge, in 1923. The present clubhouse dates from the early 1960s and, significantly for our purposes, it is loaded to the gunwales with booty.

The first things to grab one's attention are a pair of handsome marble lions, one sleeping and one ready to pounce. These are copies of Antonio Canova's sculptures which guard the tomb of Pope Clement XIII in Rome. Nearby is a clock set in the wheel of a gun carriage from Nelson's onetime flagship, HMS

Foudroyant. *Foudroyant* survived the French Revolution and the Napoleonic wars only to be run aground in 1897 whilst functioning as a tourist attraction in Blackpool. The ignominy! A more impressive piece of Nelsonalia is a telescope which belonged to one-eyed wonder.[30]

Amongst the cases of yachting trophies are the Emperor of Russia Rosebowl, made by Fabergé and presented by Tsar Nicholas II in 1909; and the huge Heligoland Cups, with their enamel portraits of Edward VII and Kaiser Wilhelm II. Kaiser Bill donated these in 1912 – his membership was terminated two years later. A dedicated room is stacked high with half-model yachts. Part library and part art instillation, this collection traces the evolution of yacht design from the middle of the nineteenth century onwards. Boating enthusiasts will no doubt find it an invaluable academic resource, but even the most scurvy landlubber can appreciate this picturesque scene. With all those brightly coloured hulls it looks like something which one might find in the Tate Modern, but far better conceived.

---

[30] The club used to have two of Nelson's telescopes, but one was trousered many moons ago.

A rarer treat is the model of the *Royal George* displayed on the quarterdeck.[31] This is one of around four hundred models united by the exceptional circumstances behind their creation, and by the materials which their craftsmen employed. These so-called "bone ships" were built by French POWs during the Napoleonic Wars. They are made with animal bones, human hair, tortoise shells, ivory, and anything else which could be bartered, scavenged, whittled, buffed, and otherwise prodded into use.

An early example of the genre, the *Royal George* was probably carved by a *marinière* held in one of the West Country prisons, such as Dartmoor, Launceston, or Exeter. It might seem peculiar that a captive should devote his time to creating a memorial to a warship belonging to his captors, but four possible reasons are advanced by way of explanation. First, he would have been terribly bored. In previous conflicts there had been an active exchange of prisoners, but Napoleon put a stop to all that, so the prisoner would have been aware that he was there for the long haul. Secondly, many of the captured combatants had been skilled

---

[31] The model *Royal George* was a gift from the New York Yacht Club, presented in 1965 as a gesture of Yanko-Brit friendship. Commodore Vanderbilt was amongst those who attended the presentation party.

craftsmen before conscription, or at least now had ample time to learn. Thirdly, as the captive's staple diet was beef or mutton – with daily rations of half a pound of this meat! – there was no shortage of animal bone to work with. Finally, one must consider the market forces. Guards would help prisoners to sell their models in special prison markets, and British ships were in greater demand than French ships. These models went for a tidy sum, and any profits could be used to purchase more building materials, or perhaps to buy those little luxuries which make life worth living.

The detail one can observe in the *Royal George* is typical of the bone ships. The hull curves gracefully outwards as it meets the decks, which are stacked with dozens of minute cannons. The forecastle sweeps toward a tiny figurehead. Three tapered masts, a thrusting bowsprit and a forest of rigging are the work of a supremely steady hand. Like most of these models, it is built of a combination of bone and wood, but unusually it also incorporates ivory. Bone planks are fixed onto outer layers of the hull, with the interior bulkheads and ribs made of wood. Its fabrication could have taken up to six months of labour. The whole thing is not more than a foot in length, but the

131

detailing is impeccable, especially when one considers that this was all completed from memory and with only the most rudimentary of tools.

What of the ship that this *marinière* chose to model? The *Royal George* in question was the fifth of eight bearing that name, commissioned into the Royal Navy between 1675 and 1911. She was a first rate of a hundred guns, launched at Chatham in 1788. She biffed the French in the Napoleonic Wars and also made an ill-fated expedition to bombard Constantinople. She was eventually broken up in 1822. It is a whimsical thought, wholly undermined by research, that after de-commissioning, she was used as a prison hulk, thereby obligingly acting as a sitter for the craftsman who created this model. It is edifying to think of something so beautiful being produced in such unpromising conditions. Loveliness from squalor, creativity in captivity, new life from old bones. You know, I think there might be a sermon in that.

18

UNIVERSITY WOMEN'S CLUB

LUCY MAKIN MURAL

"No nation but the English is capable of the social solecism of excluding women from their society as a matter of luxury." So wrote Catherine Gore, a spirited Victorian crusader against Clubland. Until relatively recently, almost all the doors of Clubland were closed to the fairer sex. Not only were women ineligible to join clubs but often they were refused entrance even as guests. As one Savilian thundered in 1952, "Not one inch past the coat pegs, not a centimetre nearer the privy. Not a woman past the barograph." The blind artist and author William Wilthew Fenn justified this policy of exclusion thusly, "A clubbable woman is an anomaly and long may she remain so." Such an analysis fails to take account of the women who were admitted alongside men as equals in Francis Dashwood's notoriously hedonistic Hellfire Club, but the slanderous untruth that all women are unclubbable long prevailed in Clubland.

Rapidly and inexorably things have changed. A majority of clubs are now co-ed, whether this has been brought about through legal insistence (as in Scotland), financial necessity and a desire to avoid negative press, or in many cases through a genuine desire amongst the membership to enjoy feminine company. Unfashionable though it sounds to modern ears, single sex clubs do perform a valuable function. There is a certain sort of man who needs the space to be comfortable in the company of other men. The barriers between the sexes have been removed so comprehensively in most areas of modern life that it seems churlish to deny such individuals this last bastion of reactionary masculinity.[32]

---

[32] In 2017, the single-sex Savile Club found itself the subject of scrutiny in the popular press when one of its members transitioned his gender from male to female. It was decided that it would be unclubbable to boot-out the person in question who had, after all, been a bloke when he was elected.

The argument cuts two ways, of course. Women are entitled to spaces in which they can be alone with other women, and this is an opinion which one hears voiced today with increasing frequency. There are petitions for women only railway carriages such as one finds in Japan. Interest in women only schools and colleges is growing. There is even a new chain of female clubs named for Madeline Albright, the former US Secretary of State who said that "there is a special place in Hell for women who don't help other women." A branch of the AllBright Club (the extra "l" has been added to avoid unwanted attention from Albright's lawyers) has now opened in Mayfair; a feminine incursion deep into enemy territory.

There has, however, long been a female outpost in Clubland. The University Women's Club was opened in 1887 and has been situated in Audley Square since 1921. It was intended to provide a comfortable space in central London for educated women to enjoy each other's company. Less chic than the AllBright Club, it is indisputably more charming.

In the early years of the last century there were several clubs which catered to the exclusively X-Chromosomed: the Pioneer, the Lyceum, the

Empress, the Alexandra, the Ladies' Carlton, Ladies' Athenaeum, and Ladies' Imperial. Respectable bourgeoise places all, fragrant with heavy Edwardian perfume. Of this roll-call only the University Women's Club still survives, owing largely to the fact that the UWC owns its clubhouse. And what a beautiful clubhouse it is. The property was formerly the residence of Lord and Lady Arthur Russell, one of Victorian London's most brilliant couples. It was Flora Russell, their daughter, who sold the property to the UWC in 1921. (Flora Russell was at one stage engaged to George Stephen, Virginia Woolf's stepbrother. Upon hearing the news of their engagement, Woolf is said to have dictated a congratulatory telegram which read, "She is an angel". The author signed the missive with her childhood nickname, "Goat". Somewhere between dictation and delivery the message got muddled, and when the telegram arrived it said, "She is an aged Goat". It was a short engagement.)

The UWC is a convivial, bright, studious club appealing predominantly to convivial, bright, studious women. It has open fires and comfortable sofas, on which comfortable members sit with open books. The walls are hung with portraits of sharp-eyed female academics and pleasant varsity watercolours. There is a small courtyard which contains a single plane tree, much loved by the members.

It is the drawing room which contains the club's most arresting feature: a chinoiserie mural of birds and flora created in the 1990s by the artist Lucy Makin. Drawing rooms and chinoiserie go together like Campari and soda, and there are some spectacular examples in the great houses of Europe.[33] Makin was only twenty-five, and still in art school, when she received this commission. Her scheme was not without its early critics. Whilst the mural was still in progress, Makin received a visit from the so-called "Girton Girls". This posse of *grandes dames* had been in the first cohort of women to take a full degree at Cambridge, and their presence loomed large at the club. The Girton Girls took umbrage at Makin's inclusion of a large cockerel in her scheme, arguing that it was too masculine a bird for the drawing room of a ladies' club. As one of these formidable women put it – in an entendre that was barely double – "we can't have a cock loose in our drawing room!" Makin had a playful solution: the cock was to be kept in his cage, where he could not trouble the members. Meanwhile

---

[33] The Chinese Room in Claydon House is the most bonkers survival in Britain.

the other little birds would be depicted flying freely about the room, liberated from their cages, the doors of which had been flung open. The visual metaphor was clear, and the resulting mural was feminine, fetching, and fanciful in the best tradition of chinoiserie.

Like so much that is appealing in European culture, the origins of chinoiserie can be traced to the House of Bourbon. Giuseppe Tomasi di Lampedusa wrote that the Bourbons were responsible for "superb architecture and revolting décor (just like the Bourbon monarchy itself)" but then he was writing from an Italian as opposed to a French perspective. Perhaps the earliest example of chinoiserie was Louis XIV's porcelain pavilion at Trianon. It was within this mock-Oriental bolthole that the Sun King made love to Madame de Montespan. The affair was not to last, and neither was the pavilion. When the mother of Louis' seven illegitimate children was replaced in the king's affections by their governess, Madame de Maintenon, this new lover declared the porcelain pavilion to be "too cold" and the structure was demolished.

The mural at the UWC declares that neither chinoiserie nor Clubland belong entirely to another age; rather, both are evolving art forms. Twenty years after she had painted the drawing room, Makin returned to the UWC to touch up her design, obscured by two decades of cigarette smoke. All the Girton Girls were now dead, but the UWC had been infused with their vigorous, feminine spirit. It is good to know that in the heart of Mayfair there is a club which caters for women, and which does so boldly, traditionally, and gracefully. Furthermore, I find it a strangely comforting thought that there is a club to which I will never belong on the grounds of my sex, rather than my general lack of appeal.

19

THE SAVILE CLUB

WILLIAM NICHOLSON

"A SAVILE CLERIC-CUES & BALLS"

The Savile's motto is *Sodalitas Convivium*. Not being a Latin scholar, I am tempted to translate this as "Unity through Fun", but the reality is less sinister. When considering candidates for membership the Savile has always been less concerned with a person's profession or position than with how successfully he will fit in with the *sodalitas* of the club. Hence Sir John Cockcroft's claim, "I take my acquaintances to the Athenaeum, but my friends to the Savile". If there is such a thing as the archetypal Savilian then Rudyard Kipling's remark about the "long-haired literati of the Savile Club" is not far off; although Oscar Wilde – prince of the long-haired literati – was put up for membership but never joined. No club is entirely bore free, and a few have even slipped through the portal of No. 69 Brook Street, but in time we trust that they will be duly "Savilised".

When Harold Nicholson wrote that Henry "Chips" Channon's home in Belgravia was "baroque and rococo and what-ho and oh-no-no" he could have been describing the Savile Club. An unremarkable exterior conceals an exquisite French interior designed for Walter Burns, an American tycoon who had the good sense to have been born in Paris. When the Savile moved into the property in 1927 aspects of this décor were considered too louche for respectable Edwardian clubmen.[34] The lavishly gilded ballroom (the only one of its kind in Clubland) was hidden beneath sober colours, and the *putti* which had danced across its powder blue ceiling were banished with censorious brushstrokes. For better or for worse we live in less Francophobic times. Happily the original exuberant scheme was reconstructed in time for the Savile's 150th anniversary in 2018. In a typically playful addition one of the resurrected cherubs now clutches in his chubby hands a bottle of the club's sesquicentennial champagne. The whole effect would be quite nauseating if it weren't executed in such good humour.[35]

The Savile's ebullient Louis XVI dining room contains a wealth of treasures. Emeric Pressburger's Oscar statuette and BAFTA trophy sit across the room from a case of glassware containing a two-thousand-year-old plate, which is as light as a napkin and as delicate as an unboiled egg. Downstairs in the member's drawing room, H.G. Wells' writing desk is now used to

---

[34] I am reminded of Augustus Carp, whose father insisted on an English pronunciation of the family home: *Mon Repos*.
[35] This anniversary was also marked by a tour around the club's former premises, led by a team of trumpeters playing a fanfare commissioned for this occasion.

support the Candidate's Book. On the second floor, in the small library known as the Monument, letters from R.L. Stevenson to his mother are displayed alongside books written and donated by the club's many scribblers. But let us leave aside these more obvious treasures and turn instead to a fraying book cover, simply framed, which depicts a stout gentleman playing snooker.

The Savile has never been a sporting club, as authors and aesthetes do not look at ease in white socks.[36] Nevertheless, a sturdy Victorian billiards table dominates the aptly-named Potter Room (so-called for Stephen Potter, author of the entertaining *Gamesmanship* books). Many clubs play snooker, but only one plays Savile Snooker. This local variation differs from the standard game in several respects. Most importantly, each player must hit a red ball at the start of the match, after which he may "volunteer" any ball he wishes. There are fewer coloured balls than in

---

[36] This said, C.B. Fry was a Savilian, and he represented England in both cricket and football, whilst also holding the world record for the long jump. Fry also purportedly turned down the throne of Albania, and tried to align the Boy Scouts with the Hitler Youth; no life is perfect.

the standard game, and these balls may be attempted out of the prescribed order.

These rules were conceived at the end of the nineteenth century to accelerate the progress of the game, allowing more Savilians the chance to play on the club's sole billiards table. There are rumours that Robert Louis Stevenson took the game with him to Samoa, where it is still played, and that Howard Carter may have introduced it to Egypt, perhaps in payment for all those treasures he pinched. At any rate, it is Stevenson who is credited with noting the relationship between proficiency at snooker and a misspent youth.[37]

The Potter Room is furnished with several striking prints executed by William Nicholson, who was known to his fellow Savilians as Billie Nick. Nicholson was an accomplished painter of society portraits, landscapes, and still life; a lithographer; a set designer; and one half of the "Beggerstaffs" along with his brother-in-law, James Pryde. Winston Churchill studied under Nicholson and lauded him as "the person who taught me most about painting". Neither overtly modernist

---

[37] Although the line was apparently uttered by Charles Roupell, a lawyer, who was a guest at the Savile, not Stevenson.

nor slavishly derivative, Nicholson's paintings have an elusive and haunting beauty. Following his death Nicholson's reputation was eclipsed by that of his fashionably experimental son Ben; until, that is, a major retrospective at the RA in 2004. Despite his artistic resurgence he is probably remembered most affectionately for illustrating the nation's favourite childhood tear-jerker, *The Velveteen Rabbit*.

Nicholson was a fixture of the Savile. When the club was still at No. 107 Piccadilly, the artist was asked to design the interior. His son recalled that he "gave the dining-room a dark blue ceiling and became fed-up with the number of members who approached him with 'What about a few stars?'. He had 'no stars' printed and pinned onto the inside of the lapel of his jacket and when he saw a member approaching him with a knowing look, he held up his hand and said 'Wait a moment' and turned the 'no stars' for the member to read."

For all his achievements, it is Nicholson's prints which mark his most unique artistic contribution. A restrained colour palette and bold lines are used to create something which is at once melancholic and humorous. In the 1920s Nicholson caricatured a selection of his fellow Savilians and bound these images in a volume. Each illustration was accompanied by a Clerihew composed by an unknown author. The caricatures include H.G. Wells standing upon a mountain of books ("Wells Sells – Hells Bells!"), and Peter Rodd – known as Prodd – a sometime Fascist and fulltime idler who was the inspiration for Evelyn Waugh's Basil Seal ("Rodd thought he was God: Now he knows that was a pose"). Some years back the book was taken apart and the images individually framed. The front cover is mounted beside the billiard table. It shows a portly priest in tall hat and shirt sleeves playing a game of Savile Snooker ("A Savile Cleric-Cues & Balls"). The image is pure Nicholson: witty, whimsical, and comically grotesque. It is a testament both to a great Edwardian artist, and to an enduring Savile tradition.

20

THE FLYFISHERS' CLUB

STATUETTE OF IZAAK WALTON

There are clubs which seek to be meeting places for diverse persons seeking good conversation and passable food in a comfortable setting. And then there are clubs where folk who share a common interest or background come together to discuss what a splendid thing it is to share that common interest or background, and to lament those persons who have different, less interesting interests, and who come from other, dissimilar backgrounds. The Flyfishers' is the Platonic ideal of this latter type of club. Its members range from the keen on fishing to the obsessive about fishing. Among the earliest members was one Dr Gowland who managed to spend £30,000 – in the 1890s! – on fishing equipment.[38] When Gowland died in 1896 he left behind 367 fishing rods and fishing flies innumerable, some of which were bequeathed to his beloved club. Let this be a cautionary tale for any readers who think that fly fishing might make a bucolic and inexpensive new hobby.[39]

The Flyfishers' have made their home in no fewer than twelve locations since the club's foundation in 1884. Issues of money and space forced these migrations in most cases, although the Luftwaffe didn't help matters when they bombed Piccadilly in 1941, utterly destroying the Flyfishers' then clubhouse at no. 36. At present they reside on the second floor of the Savile

---

[38] Roughly £3,500,000 in today's money
[39] A recent history of the club lists every book written by members of the Flyfishers'. These titles include the beguiling *Trout Heresy* (Allan, 1936); the honest *Mostly About Trout* (Aston, 1921) and the thrilling *Domesday Book of Mammoth Pike* (Buller, 1979).

148

Club, in a space once occupied by the library. Savilians do not come to their club to read books, so I suspect many are blissfully unaware that their library is now full of fishermen. It is a splendid little clubhouse; comfortable, handsomely furbished, and absolutely chock-a-block with things to admire.

There are fish, of course there are fish, but there are plenty of other items worth one's time. The flies, for example, are things of great beauty. Those used for salmon fishing come in a mesmerising array of colours, with older examples utilising feathers from exotic fowl to achieve the appropriate effect. Unlike flies for trout fishing, which seek to mimic the *insecte de jour*, those used to catch salmon work by dazzling the aquatic quarry, causing them to snap at the bait in irritation.[40] The more crafty members turn their hands to tying flies after club suppers. Given the intricacy of this process one must assume that these fellows are either an abstemious bunch, or else that they have cultivated exceptional patience during their long hours riverside. I rather suspect it is the latter.

---

[40] Like real ales, salmon flies seem often to be given names which hint at impropriety. These include: Meg in her Braws, Kinmont Willie, Silver Doctor, Dusty Miller, Hairy Mary, Garry, Stoat's Tail, and Munro's Killer.

Perhaps the most important fisherman of them all was Izaak Walton, the unofficial patron saint of anglers. The Flyfishers' possesses what it once believed was Walton's own fishing creel, stamped with his initials and dated to 1646. This pot-bellied leather fishing bag was purchased by a naval chaplain from a curiosity shop near to Westminster Abbey in 1891, for the then princely sum of £29. 10s. Sadly, it is now generally accepted that the creel is an elaborate forgery from a later date. For this reason, we shall focus our attentions upon a silver statuette of Walton, which makes an elegant centrepiece on the club table. Made in Sheffield, the statuette was presented by the retiring president, Major-General Sir Victor Couper, K.C.B in 1924.

Walton was a man of letters, despite having received only a rudimentary education. Unfriendly critics commented that Walton was "rather literate than learned" but a pleasing style has ensured his enduring appeal. Walton lived near St Dunstan-in-the-West in the City of London. Here he became a friend and fishing companion to the vicar, John Donne. When Donne died in 1631, Walton composed *An Elegie* to accompany the publishing of his late friend's poetry, and later wrote an account of the poet priest's life.

Living through the chaos of the English Civil War and its beastly puritan aftermath, Walton remained a committed royalist and high churchman, despite the attendant dangers of holding such convictions. A consummate fisherman, Walton's silent hours by the river left him unprepared for the mission he accepted at the age of 58. After the Royalist defeat at the Battle of Worcester, Walton received an urgent summons from a friend who had retrieved from the battlefield one of the Crown Jewels, the so-called Lesser George. To save the precious trinket from falling into the hands of Cromwell's soldiers, Walton was charged with smuggling it back to London, from whence it could be shipped to the exiled Charles II. Despite finding the highways overrun with Cromwell's lackeys, who would surely have hanged Walton for treason had they discovered his cargo, the fisherman was successful in his mission and the Lesser George remains in the royal collection to this day.

Derring-do aside, Walton is best known for his book *The Compleat Angler*, first published in 1653, and it is for this reason that his image rests upon the Flyfishers' dining table. In *The Compleat Angler*, Walton uses fictional characters to write about fishing as equal parts philosophy, recreation, social bonding, and environmental conservation. The book is compendious, drawing on sources ranging from Pliny to Bacon to give readers the facts of fish and fishing. Remarkably, *The Compleat Angler* has been through over four hundred editions since Walton first put pen to paper, and is still available from all good bookshops, as well as some disappointing ones.

In an act of the most commendable sort of nerdishness, the curator of the Flyfishers' wrote to the membership in 2014 of his concern that their statuette carried an anachronistic rod, "complete with rod rings and reel – items that were not available to Izaak!" A silversmith was commissioned to create something more in keeping with the "hedgerow branch rod with line-winder" that Walton would have used. It is this sort of story that restores one's shattered faith in humanity. Not for nothing did Our Lord choose fishermen to be His first disciples. If ever I am elected Pope then I shall declare Izaak Walton a saint, and the Flyfishers' Club a minor basilica.

21

THE ORIENTAL CLUB

EIGHTEENTH CENTURY WATER PIPE

Oxford Street is London at its worst. Oxford Street is *anywhere* at its worst. A roiling mess of designer stubble and bootleg Gucci shuffling through soulless emporia of technicoloured nothings. The babel-noise of a thousand tongues masks the screams of those gone mad with the hatefulness of it all. How sweet, then, is that moment, when having fought the crowds with elbow and sharpened winkle-picker, one reaches the end of Stratford Place and enters the marbled hush of Stratford House. Once home to Russian royalty and haunted by a lovelorn ghost, this Adamesque mansion has been the home of the Oriental Club since 1962.

Stratford House is one of the great clubhouses of London. There are frescoed ceilings and chimney pieces supported by classical figures, and portraits of nabobs hanging on oak panelled walls. A subtler pleasure is the Calcutta Light Horse Bar, a relatively recent attempt at an informal bar and restaurant. Its lazy ceiling fans and swivelling bar stools import the ambiance of a languishing colonial club in some far-flung outpost of empire. The Calcutta Light Horse Bar makes me want to slip into a crumpled white linen suit and sit at the bar, sweating.

The Oriental Club was founded in 1824 for "Noblemen and gentlemen associated with the administration of our Eastern empire, or who have travelled or resided in Asia, at St. Helena, in Egypt, at the Cape of Good Hope, the Mauritius, or at Constantinople." The club's founding fathers have been described as a "tanned, polyglot group [who] had travelled half the world, watched widows burn by the sacred Ganges, tasted the furnace of Indian spice, commanded thousands of men and parlayed with princes in golden throne rooms." Hardly the Milton Keynes Amateur Bowls Club, then.

British intercourse with the Orient is not what it was, and today the Oriental Club has lost its boisterous edge. At weekends the quiet is positively sepulchral, making it just the place to sleep-off Friday night's hangover. The kitchen maintains its reputation for serving an absolutely belting curry, which as assets go is hard to knock.

As one would expect, the club's bibelots reflect its Eastern roots. These include a great many Indian elephants, an animal which the Oriental has adopted as its emblem. The largest of these *Proboscidea* greets members from its plinth by the front door. It was presented to the club in 1904 by a man named Tarrett Fleming, who claimed to have found it in a rubbish heap near London Docks.

There are a few other treasures of note. Outside the coffee room is a chair which once belonged to Tipu Sultan, the so-called Tiger of Mysore. Tipu was the scourge of the East India Company, rebuffing attempts to expand British influence into his kingdom. Visitors to London's V&A can marvel at "Tipu's Tiger", a near life-sized semi-automaton of an Indian tiger mauling a British soldier, with realistic death cries produced by an organ concealed in the animal's body. One does not need a doctorate in semiotics to decode that piece of propaganda. A portrait of Tipu hangs in the Oriental near to his chair, and in the members' bar there is a painting of Lord Cornwallis receiving the sultan's sons as hostages, painted by Mather Brown in 1831. One critic of the picture has noted obscurely, "Later, Brown went mad."

Despite this rich seam of exotica I have chosen to lower the tone by focussing on a gruesome object in the gentlemen's lavatories. Before relocating to Stratford House, the Oriental occupied a purpose-built clubhouse in Hanover Square. This building was demolished the day after the Oriental relocated, but a little bit of its fabric has been installed in the ground-floor loos of the new clubhouse. It takes to new heights (or should that be new depths?) the British tradition of providing something vulgar for guests to enjoy when visiting the smallest room.

This is a six foot section of a Georgian water pipe which was donated by a member in 1915. It is unambiguously phallic. Perhaps the committee felt this bequest was akin to receiving a hideous picture from a benevolent but certifiably insane uncle. "Where can we put it that won't hurt his feelings but won't upset the other members?" The giver of the pipe supposed it to be "about 200 years old". This is indeed when Hanover Square began to be developed (from 1713), as a residential address for Richard Lumley, 1st Earl of Scarbrough; one of the Immortal Seven who invited William of Orange to depose the popish James II.

Although the wooden pipe is blackened and gnarled, it can be identified as the trunk of an elm, bored through from end to end. Elm was a popular choice for water pipes as the trees grow tall and straight and, unlike other woods, it does not decay when kept permanently wet. One end of the trunk was tapered, as our specimen demonstrates, so that it could slot neatly into the next trunk. The pipes were lashed together with leather straps and, *voila!* something approximating fresh water could be pumped from limpid streams into the festering heart of London.

By the late eighteenth century, London's water supply system was the envy of the world; more than eighty percent of the city's houses had piped water. Voltaire became an unlikely student of London's domestic water supply during his exile from Paris in the 1720s. Alongside his commentaries on the English constitution, the philosopher found time to write on the subject to a friend back home, "I wish that all the houses of Paris had water like those in London do." Even elm rots eventually, and the Georgian water pipes could not accommodate London's burgeoning population. The Victorians removed most of them, though some, like our example, survived into the Edwardian era. Whilst this lumpen piece of pipe is far from the most beautiful of the Oriental's treasures, it is a gratifying object to find in the lavatory.

22

BUCK'S CLUB

SIR JOHN WILLOUGHBY'S DECOUPAGE SCREEN

Buck's Club seems to belong more to the eighteenth century than to our own beastly age, which is impressive given that it was only founded in 1919. Wood-panelled and modestly-proportioned, Buck's is the sort of beefsteak and claret concern in which Charles James Fox might feel at home. It is a club that has no vegetarian items on its menu, and which thinks that veganism is a disease brought back from the Congo. Its very name adds to the illusion of pedigree, suggesting that it came of age with those other confidently monosyllabic clubs, Brooks's and White's.

This antique atmosphere should not be thought to imply stolidity. Not for nothing did Mr Wodehouse use Buck's as the model for Bertie Wooster's Drones Club.[41] Whilst diners are unlikely to find themselves pelted by bread rolls, a certain high-spiritedness is signified by the cricket stumps painted on the bar. As the wear and tear to the wood testifies, this is no art installation.

Speaking of the bar at Buck's, it would be remiss not to reference the club's great contribution to Western civilisation; *viz*, the Buck's Fizz. Just as Iberians

---

[41] Waugh's "Brat's Club" is also an obvious mirror-image of Buck's.

shudder to think of that bottle of cream sherry congealing in Great Aunty Glenda's pantry, so the barmen of Buck's must gaze off mournfully each Christmas Day at the thought of all those glasses of cava and orange-juice-drink masquerading as Buck's Fizz. The cocktail apparently began as an attempt to mimic a Bellini, a drink for which British officers had developed a taste whilst in Italy. English barmen in 1919 did not have access to a ready supply of peach puree, but orange juice was easier to come by.[42] The substitution was a great success and Buck's became a place of pilgrimage for sots the world over.

The clubhouse contains some nice bits and pieces, but in keeping with the general aesthetic there is nothing too showy. There is a sweet little bust of HM the Queen Mother, smiling a benediction on the club's activities. A raffish portrait of the club's founder, Herbert Buckmaster, hangs in the bar.[43] Perhaps in memory of seedy weekends long past a model of the Vivid, the

---

[42] Samuel Pepys drank the first recorded glass of orange juice in England in 1669.

[43] The irascible "Buck" continued to live in the club which bore his name well into his ninth decade, no doubt adding to the private house atmosphere. He was an eccentric and an autocrat rather than a businessman, and when – in 1966 – Buckmaster finally went to meet his maker, members had to reach deeply into their pockets to stop the perennially mismanaged club from closing.

stagecoach which once ran between London and Brighton, is nestled in an alcove above the gallery.

Perhaps the *strangest* object in Buck's is hidden on the second floor, away from the hubbub of club life. I say strange both because it seems out of place in a gentlemen's club, and also because of how and why this item came into existence. I am referring to a late nineteenth century decoupage folding screen, presented to Buck's by Mr and Mrs Edward Dawe. One side utilises military and other traditionally masculine images. The reverse features hundreds – perhaps thousands – of pictures of women, some in a state of undress, which gives the piece a strong whiff of sexpestery.

This remarkable object was the creation of Sir John Willoughby, an officer in the Royal Horse Guards. Handsome, sporting, and aristocratic (he was the fifth and final Baronet of Baldon House), Willoughby's military exploits were well reported in the popular press. He served in Egypt in the 1880s, Matabeleland in 1893, and later in South Africa. At the Relief of Mafeking he was raised to the rank of major. A low point in Willoughby's career came at the end of 1895, when he played a leading part in the Jameson Raid; an ill-judged incursion of British soldiers into territory controlled by the South African Republic. It was hoped that this show of British military strength would stir up anti-Boer feeling, and would ultimately help to extend British influence over the Transvaal. The Raid was a failure and an embarrassment for Britain. The locals did not rise up, and Cecil Rhodes, who had supported the incursion, was sacked as premier of the Cape Colony.

Rhodes was not the only one to suffer because of the blunder; the leaders of the Raid were thrown into gaol. Amongst the guilty was Sir John Willoughby, who decided to occupy his time behind bars by constructing the creepiest folding screen in Christendom. Willoughby had wood imported specially from Rhodesia, and apparently had access to no end of girly mags. Having completed his project, Willoughby presented the screen to Queen Alexandra, wife of Edward VII. Her Majesty's reaction upon being presented with this gift is not recorded, but it is worth noting that the screen did not remain in her family's possession, but passed through two further pairs of hands before arriving at Buck's. Probably better that it is kept here than in a private home; it is the sort of thing which gives house guests the wrong impression.

23

BLACKS CLUB

DIVAN

Blacks is a different sort of club. This becomes apparent as soon as one passes through its notorious black portal on Dean Street to be greeted first by a heavy black curtain and then by an androgynous European wearing the sort of trousers which turn a tenor into a falsetto. Ushered into the parlour on a quiet mid-winter mid-afternoon, a fire burns in the grate and the soft muzak is interrupted by the nee-naw of a police car pulling up opposite. A little reminder of a former, seedier Soho, before the organic cobblers and vegan cheesemongers moved into town.[44]

Blacks is trendy. Achingly, panic-attack-inducingly hip. Normally, clubs and trendiness go together like toddlers and sharp corners. A club which chases the gaudy baubles of contemporary acclaim is doomed to slide into irrelevance when its architects find themselves on the wrong side of forty. And yet, much as it pains me to say it, Blacks works. It *is* cool. It has *remained* cool since its foundation deep in the analogue mists of the early 1990s despite – inevitably – some questionable management decisions. Blacks was the creation of the outrageous Tom Bantock, formerly a gentleman poacher and latterly an intense, self-mythologizing Soho "character". Banned from the Groucho Club for setting fire to a casual acquaintance, Bantock ran Blacks as his personal fiefdom. In those early years, Bantock could be seen prowling about like

---

44 Blacks is opposite the site of the former Colony Room Club; the low drinking club once frequented by Francis Bacon and Jeffrey Bernard.

a cartoon alley cat, identifiable by a vivid neck scar, supposedly sustained during a barroom brawl and sewed up by his own hands.

Blacks was intended as an archly knowing inversion of White's, London's oldest and most prestigious club. At Blacks there are no snoring viscounts in hairy tweeds, nor braying city boys comparing pay-packets, and certainly no soporific prelates boring on about their archdeacons. Blacks is for the Soho plutocracy: visual artists, media moguls, opinion formers, and other varieties of the chronically useless. Yet unlike the Groucho Club or Soho House, part of Blacks' appeal is that it has retained enough of a more traditional club to make the joke work. Blacks is recognisably a club in the great Clubland tradition. It is located in an elegant Georgian townhouse, built in 1732 by John Meard Jnr, an apprentice of Sir Christopher Wren. Like more traditional clubs, Blacks promises conviviality and conversation within a self-selecting crowd. Like the clubs of Pall Mall there are rooms set aside for drinking, dining, and reading. Being Soho there are also spaces provided for groping, frotting, and petting. Blacks works precisely because it is not revolutionary, but is rather a witty and roguish reimagining of a known type.

Blacks' Dean Street clubhouse manages to be both smart (Farrow and Ball paint) and silly (a bath tub full of wine). Most rooms have working fireplaces and high ceilings, providing cosiness without being cramped. The club's art collection is eclectic. There are engravings by Hogarth, displaying the sort of good natured Georgian depravity which Blacks seeks to recreate. These hang alongside a selection of lurid canvasses splattered with trippy cosmic chunder. There are regular rotating art and photographic installations of varying quality. Taken as a whole it is an invigorating combination.

The possession that really sums up Blacks is a filthy bed which occupies a small room on the second floor. That bed has seen some naughtiness in its time; I don't know how it sleeps at night. I was once wrestled onto it by a Knight of Malta during a gathering of the now sadly defunct Trouser Club (*floreat trousum*), but that story shall have to wait for my memoirs.[45]

The placing of a bed in a reception room is hardly a novel concept. In ancient times aristocratic Greeks and Romans would recline on divans to eat their porcupine heart truffles and sparrow beak soufflés.

---

[45] Or until I am bought a drink.

Dining horizontally sounds like it would invite indigestion, but those ancient blue bloods were made of sturdier stuff than us moderns. A more recent manifestation is the daybed or *chaise longue* (the Americans call this item a "chaise lounge", which is inexcusable.) The daybed was intended originally as a resting place for convalescents, but was adopted in the Georgian period by genteel women who wished to receive visitors to their boudoirs in a state of repose. The *chaise longue* is incurably louche. Although today more likely to be seen in the sitting room of a respectable maiden aunt, a *chaise longue* seems incomplete without powdered and periwigged gentlefolk strewn languidly upon it.

Later in the nineteenth century the practical-minded Victorians resurrected the daybed as the "fainting couch" for corseted women seeking a comfortable place to swoon, but at Blacks the hedonistic Georgian ideal is maintained. In our own late capitalist age, where size most certainly matters, Blacks has supersized their divan so that it fills the small room in which it is set. A few years ago Blacks held an artistic exhibition in homage to Hogarth entitled "The Rake and the Harlot". Projected above the bed were the exhibition's titular characters, engaging in what appeared to be a mutually satisfying act of shared concupiscence. Whilst Blacks has gone through several changes of management in recent years, and is keen to attract a younger clientele, the bed has remained a constant feature of this distinctly Soho outpost of Clubland.

24

THE GARRICK CLUB

HENRY IRVING BY JOHN EVERETT MILLAIS

In Clubland's nascent years, actors were considered unfit company for more respectable persons. David Garrick was himself the subject of a withering snub by Dr Johnson, the Ur-Clubman, when the former expressed his interest in joining Johnson's Literary Club. "I love my little David dearly – better than all or any of his flatterers do", said Johnson to Henry Thrale, "but surely one ought to sit in a society like ours

'unelbowed by a gamester, pimp, or player.'"[46] Alas, poor Garrick! So when the Garrick Club was founded in 1831 as a place where "actors and men of refinement and education might meet on equal terms", it was

---

[46] Johnson here quotes Pope.

intended both as a posthumous vindication for Garrick, and an expansion of Clubland's horizons beyond its early literary and aristocratic boundaries.

The Garrick remains a haven for thespians seeking to be among their own kind, free from the intrusions of autograph hunters and their mutant offspring, the selfie-takers. The handsome West End clubhouse, located within stumbling distance of London's theatre district, wears its heritage with pride. Each nook, and almost every cranny, displays some assemblage of theatrical memorabilia. An impressive library contains over ten thousand items. Alongside the books there are valuable manuscripts, playbills, theatre programmes, and scrapbooks containing rare archival clippings.

Even more impressive is the Garrick's art collection, which includes over a thousand paintings, drawings, and sculptures. It is the largest theatrical art collection in the world. An 1890 history says that "the Garrick is indeed a picture gallery in itself", so extensive is its collection and of such fine quality. In the thin years of the late 1960s and 70s, the Garrick was rumoured to have been selling some of these pictures to make ends meet. This was before the club had an extraordinary spot of good luck, courtesy of the late A.A. Milne. Upon his death in 1956, Milne left the rights to his much-loved *Pooh* books to four beneficiaries: his family, the Royal Literary Fund, Westminster School, and the Garrick. This bought the club a steady trickle of income, until the Disney Corporation lifted Winnie out of his picturesque obscurity and made him a global megastar. In 2001 the Garrick sold its portion of Milne's estate to Disney for what Pooh might have called "a goloptious full-up pot of honey", and the fate of the club's art collection was secured.[47]

Amidst all these treasures, one picture seems to capture the spirit and history of the club. It concerns two of the nineteenth century's leading figures in the fields of painting and theatre respectively, who cultivated a firm friendship within the Garrick. The Pre-Raphaelite Brotherhood met often at the club. John Everett Millais was the finest painter of the

---

[47] In 1998 the *Independent* pondered whether Winnie the Pooh might be accepted as a member of the Garrick. "On the plus side, he is male, he is hairy and he has an oral fetish of the most rampant sort. On the minus side, he is a bear." This latter point need not necessarily be considered a drawback. In 1885 the Tavern Club of Boston USA purchased a performing bear cub from a visiting circus. This period as a one-bear menagerie was cut short following the reaction of Julius, the club servant, to the suggestion that he might don "a highly picturesque Spanish costume for the special purpose of leading the bear on a chain onto the Common and exercising him there."

bunch and the first to join the club, being elected to membership in 1855. Millais was an excellent draughtsman and less mawkishly sentimental than the other Pre-Raphaelite's (*exempli gratia* Holman Hunt's viciously ugly "May Morning"). Later in his career Millais diversified his style with what we might charitably judge to be mixed results. He was, however, a tremendous portraitist. Millais' portrait of Henry Irving, the greatest actor of the Victorian age, is a typically incisive character study.

Henry Irving was born in 1838 as John Henry Brodribb. One can see why he thought the change of name necessary if he was to achieve success in a notoriously shallow profession. Brodribb adopted the new moniker partly due to his admiration for the romances of Washington Irving, and partly due to his interest in the sermons of the otherworldly Scottish preacher Edward Irving, whose later followers, in what became the Catholic Apostolic Church, believed that when Christ returned it would be to say Mass in Gordon Square.

After years of hard slog in provincial theatre, the man who now called himself Henry Irving found fame in an 1871 production of *The Bells*, staged at London's

Lyceum Theatre. This tale of a murderer haunted by the ghost of his victim suited Irving's talent for the melodramatic. (It is said that Irving was the inspiration for Bram Stoker's *Dracula*; Stoker had been Irving's PA, and looked upon his employer as "a god"). Not that Irving's histrionics were reserved for the stage. As the actor and his wife rode back in their brougham after the triumphant opening night of *The Bells* she asked him, "Are you going to go on making a fool of yourself like this all your life?" An enraged Irving signalled to the driver to stop, removed himself from the carriage and walked away; he never saw or spoke to his wife again.

Remarkably, Irving was blackballed on his first attempt to join the Garrick. Recent research has revealed that the blackballer in question was a fellow actor, resentful of what appeared to be the overnight success of this arresting new talent. Jealousy has always been a besetting sin of actors. One imagines that when Thespis first stepped out from the chorus line, dissenting voices grumbled that he was getting too big for his sandals. Irving was persuaded to submit his name again and his page in the candidate's book, plastered in more than fifty signatures, can be seen framed in the club's hallway. The original page with the infamous blackball is preserved behind.[48]

After each performance, Irving would arrive at the Garrick near to midnight, to eat and to hold forth in the small dining room which he favoured. In 1895, Irving became the first actor to be knighted for his achievements, ushering in a new standard of social respectability for what had long been considered a vulgar and frivolous profession. (In the medieval ranking of all created matter known as the Great Chain of Being, actors were classed alongside pirates, and only slightly above slugs and gravel). For a club which was synonymous with the theatre, Irving's honour was also an honour for the Garrick.

Irving's luck ran out later in life, and he returned to touring provincial theatres. In 1905, he suffered a stroke whilst performing a show in Bradford. Whether or not it was simply the shock of finding himself in Bradford we shall never know. The ailing actor was taken to the lobby of the nearby Midland Hotel where he died shortly afterwards. The chair on which he had

---

[48] On blackballing see Chapter 33, "The Norfolk Club"

been sitting was purchased by a member of the Garrick and presented to the club, where it remains to this day.

Millais' portrait was commissioned by the Garrick to commemorate Irving's knighthood. It was paid for by subscription of the membership. Not only were artist and subject both members of the club, but so too was T.O. Barlow, who presented a frame bearing the Garrick's Shakespearian motto, "All the World's a Stage".[49]

Irving was thrilled with the result, but his opinion was not widely shared. The illustrator Harry Furniss, who spent decades studying Irving for *Punch* and the *Illustrated London News*, sniffed that "Millais' portrait... gives one no idea of strength, and Irving had a strong face. And as he frequently sat under this portrait it was easy to contrast the original with the picture." Ellen Terry thought Irving's enthusiasm for the portrait typically misguided: "Henry had a strange affection for the wrong pictures of himself. He disliked the Bastien Lepage, the Whistler, and the Sargent, which never even saw the light. He adored the weak,

---

[49] The carver of the frame took Barlow to court (unsuccessfully) over non-payment, with Millais ready to be called upon as a witness.

handsome picture by Millais". However, the weakness which is written across Irving's face is, I think, testimony to Millais' perspicacious, and his deep friendship with the actor who would be a pallbearer at his funeral. The portrait captures how Irving's affectedness, his thespish insouciance, masked an inner melancholy. Millais espied Irving's inner Brodribb, and this is what he painted. The result is a picture both theatrical and personal; a fitting testimony to its subject and to his beloved Garrick Club.

25

THE BEEFSTEAK CLUB

GRIDIRON

It used to be said that the Beefsteak was so exclusive that its members needed to be "a relation of God, and a damned close relation at that". There is an old story, apparently true in part, which illustrates the point. In nineteen-o-something the Beefsteak was raided by police following a tip that it was the front for a brothel.

An inspector gained entry and found four respectable looking gentlemen dining at a long table.

"And who might you be?" demanded the inspector of the first man.

"I am the Lord Chancellor", came the reply.

"Aha! And you, sir?"

"The Archbishop of Canterbury."

"Oh yes, and the next?"

"I am the Governor of the Bank of England"

"And I suppose you are the Prime Minister?"

"As a matter of fact, I am", replied Arthur Balfour.

The Earl of Kintore was guilty of exaggeration when he suggested that members have either to be "a peer who has learned to read and write or a journalist who has learned table manners." To be a Beefsteak one needs principally to be able to talk, and to know when not to talk shop. The centrepiece of the club is a long table, and diners are seated in the order in which they arrive, so that it is impossible to know whom you may have as your dining companion. New members are still told the salutary tale of the young man, not recognising his neighbour, who lectured Rudyard Kipling about how to write short stories.

The Beefsteak's clubhouse on Irving Street is modest by the standards of Clubland. There are a couple of bedrooms for country members, but the main body of the club is a single room furnished with prints of old members, the long table, and a few ubiquitous leather armchairs. The principal treasure on display links the Beefsteak Club of today to a more venerable foundation. This is one of the holy relics of Clubland: the original gridiron of the Sublime Society of Beefsteaks. It is a stark and emaciated object, blackened and slightly crooked.

The Sublime Society was founded around the year 1735, although details of its inception are hard to come by. In variations on the same theme, the harlequin John Rich and the painter George Lambert are both credited with having founded the club. Both stories revolve around the Theatre Royal in Covent Garden, of which Rich was the manager and Lambert employed as a scene painter. In the earliest recorded version, Lambert took to cooking in his studio, being too busy to eat elsewhere. Stout fellow that he was, Lambert favoured grilled beef and plenty of it. Soon the enticing odours emanating from the studio began to attract the attention of others around the theatre, and Lambert took to sharing his beef with those who stopped by. It was suggested that these meals become a regular affair, and so the Sublime Society was born; Lambert's gridiron became its emblem.

Twenty years later *The Connoisseur*, a London weekly, described how "the most ingenious artists in the kingdom meet every Saturday in a noble room at the top of Covent-Garden theatre, and never suffer any dish except Beef-steaks to appear". Membership was limited to twenty-four and drawn from the leading artists, actors, and musicians of the day. Early members included William Hogarth and Samuel Johnson. A smattering of royalty added respectability.

The Sublime Society was boisterous rather than depraved. It employed elaborate regalia and rituals, intended as an irreverent parody of masonry. Members wore a whiggish uniform of blue jacket and buff waistcoat, with brass buttons stamped with the gridiron and the motto "BEEF AND LIBERTY". The club's officers included the President for the Day, the Bishop, the Recorder, and Boots. The President was selected by rota, and was invested with a special gridiron badge. His ceremonial headwear included a tricorn wrongly believed to have belonged to David Garrick, a plume, and a Beefeater's hat. The plume had to be worn and then swiftly removed when putting forth a resolution. The Bishop was charged with singing the anthem and pronouncing the grace. Boots was always the club's most junior member. A general dogsbody charged with waiting on the others, if Boots showed any signs of discontent with his treatment then he was marched out of the room by two members carrying halberds and a third with a ceremonial sword, and ticked-off by the Recorder. He was then wrapped in the garment of repentance (the tablecloth) and permitted to return. The Duke of Sussex was Boots between 1808 and 1809, and was bullied spectacularly by the other members.

The original clubhouse burned down in 1808. What was supposedly Lambert's original gridiron was found in the wreckage, miraculously preserved. The gridiron was displayed in the Sublime Society's new clubhouse at the Old Lyceum Theatre until 1830, when that building also burned down. Whether these fires had anything to do with the drunken grilling of beef is not recorded. The theatre was rebuilt in 1838, with a special suite of rooms for the Beefsteaks. The gridiron which had once again been rescued from the charred remains of the former clubhouse now formed the centre ornament of the dining room ceiling. Soon after this latest move the Sublime Society of Beefsteaks began to lose its vigour. The Victorians looked askance at the frivolous rituals of the eighteenth century clubs. After two decades of decline the Sublime Society was wound up in 1867. The club's original dining table, which had somehow also survived the fire, was bought by White's Club where it remains to this day.

The current Beefsteak Club was founded nine years after the Sublime Society grilled its last steak. Shorn of faux-masonic ceremonies, the Beefsteak still has its quirks, notably that its waiters are all called Charles. It is still dedicated to the consumption of beef; Baron von Eckardstein once ate twenty-three plates of cold meat in a single sitting. The Beefsteak's clubhouse on Irving Street was purpose built, and a design of gridirons is cleverly interposed into the high pitched roof. There are a few knick-knacks of note, including some pieces of silver from the old Sublime Society. Squire Bancroft gave a silver cockerel which looks well. The club's greatest treasure is the gridiron that tradition says once belonged to George Lambert. It is a link to Clubland's raucous nascent days, before the deadening hand of respectability wagged its censorious finger and hushed the sound of silliness for silliness' sake.

26

THE NATIONAL LIBERAL CLUB

GLADSTONE'S AXE

There is a well-worn scrap of Clubland folklore involving F.E. Smith: staunch Tory, First Earl of Birkenhead, and perhaps the only friend of Winston Churchill who could drink the great man under the table. Apparently Smith was in the habit of popping into the conveniently-located National Liberal Club on his way to the House of Lords.[50] One day a porter plucked up the courage to ask this enemy of Liberalism why he felt he could freely gain admission to a club of which he was not a member. Smith responded: "Good God! Is it a club? I thought it was a public lavatory." Arf arf.

There *is* something lavatorial about the Nat. Lib.; it's the brown and green tiles which have been employed so liberally (and in such a club how else would they be employed?) by Alfred Waterhouse. In the 1960s the club whitewashed the offending tiles to try and shake the association, but today the paint is gone and the porters rather enjoy telling Birkenhead's little joke.

Tiles aside, the National Liberal occupies one of the most monumental clubhouses this side of the Atlantic.[51] It is ponderous and overwrought, and gloriously late Victorian. It used to be very much bigger, but parts have been ceded to an hotel next door, and the Savage Club occupies a little room on the ground floor.[52] In the midst of all the period flummery is an elegant free-standing marble staircase, the

---

[50] Although this story has also been linked to the Athenaeum.
[51] It was one of the first buildings in Britain to make significant structural use of steel.
[52] See Chapter 28.

largest of its type in Europe, floating majestically in the central rotunda. It replaced an earlier staircase modelled on that in the Barbarini Palace, which was destroyed by a bomb in 1941.

The National Liberal was conceived as a sort of "people's palace"; a demotic alternative to the Reform Club, open to any man who marched under the banner of popular liberalism. The moral tone of the club was set by W.E. Gladstone, who laid the foundation stone on the 4th November 1884. Gladstone asked his audience: "what are the clubs of London? I am afraid little else than temples of luxury and ease. This, however, is a club of a very different character".

Gladstone's imprint is everywhere. Extracts from his speeches are inscribed like magic runes above doorways to frighten off stray Tories. He scowls that terrible scowl from effigies innumerable. Most unsettling is the vast statue carved by Onslow Ford, which faces out across the coffee room. Members must live in fear that, like Pygmalion's ivory woman, this idol might be animated by some passing goddess, and begin wagging his marble finger at those who have been tempted to take a little wine with their pork chop.[53]

In the (now smoke-free) smoking room there is a little shrine to the Grand Old Man, maintained day and night by acolytes and vestal virgins. Within this holy of holies one may find Gladstone's venerable axe, presented to the club in 1922 by a scion of his line, and today venerated as a secondary relic by members of the Liberal Democratic Party.

Gladstone's love of tree-felling for sport is well known. He adopted the hobby as a young man, and returned to it whenever he escaped to the country. The hobby soon took on a political dimension. This axe-wielding became a metaphor for Gladstone's vigour for reform; his earnest desire to cut away at the privileges of the landowning class, and to root out injustice. Supporters flocked in their droves to the Gladstone family estate in North Wales, seeking to collect wood chippings from felled trees. The deluge of souvenir hunters grew so great that there was instituted a system whereby a

---

[53] Lewis Carol despised William Ewart Gladstone, and used to enjoy anagrammatising his name. One of Carol's best was "Will tear down all images?"

fragment of wood could only be obtained on receipt of a voucher available at the prime minister's office.

The legendary rivalry between Disraeli and **Gladstone** even extended to matters arboreal. Disraeli was a dendrophile, noting in 1860, "When I come to Hughenden I pass the first week in sauntering about my park and examining all the trees". It is not beyond the realms of possibility that Gladstone took to chopping trees in order to make Disraeli's life a little less joyful.[54]

By the end of his career, Gladstone had accrued a great collection of axes, presented to him by supporters and visiting dignitaries. These range from a razor-sharp machete to a novelty gift from the Prince and Princess of Wales in the form of a silver pencil, shaped like an axe, for the purpose of "axing questions". Most of these axes remain in Gladstone's study at Hawarden, the so-called "Temple of Peace".

The National Liberal has expanded its catchment in recent decades. This is completely understandable. After all, if the club limited its membership to card-carrying Liberal Democrats then the total number

---

[54] On Disraeli and Clubland, see Chapter 10.

could fit happily in a single *en suite* bedroom. The club's founding principles have not been completely forgotten, however. It welcomes as potential members only those who promise "not use the club's facilities for any political activities adverse to Liberalism." This sets the bar low, as Liberalism in the twenty-first century has become an indefinite proposition. Short of re-enacting the Nuremberg Rally in the smoking room I suspect you'd be beyond reproach. Say what you like about Gladstone, and I frequently do, but at least he was a true liberal in the classic sense. God only knows what the old bore would make of the politicians who claim his mantle today. Thankfully, we shall never have to find out.

27

THE SAVAGE CLUB

OLD ODELL'S CHAIR

"Bohemia", wrote one misty-eyed Edwardian, "is not the name of a country... but is that of a condition, a state of mind and heart, the outward expression of a temperament that revels in the joy of life." Bohemia was dissipated and indolent, intemperate and tolerant. It cared little for class or race or sexuality. Aristocrats and adventurers, chorus-girls and emigres mingled unselfconsciously. Above all, it was unserious. Bohemia was left much depleted by the horrors of the first world war, and further marginalised by the rise of middle-class respectability in the mid-twentieth century. No longer a potent force, Bohemia's enemies were content to let the revelries continue in corners of London, such as Soho and Chelsea, left unvisited by decent citizens. This uneasy truce came to an end in the 1980s, when those who wished to transform London into a family-friendly theme park waged total war on what remained of Bohemia. A pincer movement was launched from the politically-correct on one side, and the purveyors of chain restaurants and sanitised public spaces on the other. Bohemians are not warriors, and this most recent blow has proved damn near fatal.

Amidst all this destruction, the Savage Club remains a strong fortress of old London bohemianism. The members, who refer to each other as "Brother Savage", are a hard-drinking, often raucous bunch. The club's emblem is a Native American chief brandishing a tomahawk. This outlandishness is only emphasised by the fact that the Savage currently resides on the ground floor of the National Liberal, one of the more abstemious and progressive London clubs.[55]

Founded in 1853, the Savage began as a gathering of literary men. It arose under the leadership of the great Victorian journalist, George Augustus Sala. Whilst Sala is best remembered for his foreign and war correspondence, he also found time to publish a pornographic novel of flagellation erotica entitled *The Mysteries of Verbena House* under the pseudonym *Etonensis*. Sala's "club of merry fellows" could not at first agree on a name which captured their particular literary flavour. Various suggestions were thrown about, such as The Addison, The Johnson, or The Goldsmith. However, when somebody was so bold as to suggest The Shakespeare another member cried out in frustration, "Don't let's be pretentious. If we must have a name let it be a modest one." A third member thereby suggested "The Savage", Richard Savage having been a notorious producer of squalid verse whose greatest claim to fame was that he had once killed a man in a brawl. The name was generally agreed to be a sound one, and so the Savage Club was born in October 1857.

---

[55] See Chapter 27

From the start the Savage found it difficult to settle, and in its long and uproarious history it has pinged around every corner of Clubland. The final of these moves, to their current home in Westminster, was the latest in a series of downsizes. The club today is reduced to the bare necessities for convivial life, which is to say a bar, with use of the Nat. Lib's dining facilities.

As with an elderly relative who is forced to leave a large house for the convenience of a bungalow, this most recent relocation has left the Savage with a great deal more art and furniture than they can tastefully display. Commendably, rather than seeing this as an opportunity for a clear-out, the Savages have stuffed their single room with as much clutter as it can take, and then a bit more. Much of the wall-space is covered by menus from the club's legendary house dinners, known originally as merrifications.

Two Savages who excelled in very different fields are commemorated in the clubhouse: Sir Alexander Fleming's Nobel Medal can be seen in a display case, and Sir Charlie Chaplin's cane hangs above the bar. Other famous Savages have included James McNeill Whistler, Sir Henry Irving, Sir Edward Elgar, J.M.

Barrie, P.G. Wodehouse, and more royal dukes than you could, in good conscience and without fear of committing treason, shake a stick at.

Compared to these luminaries, it may seem strange that the member whose memory looms largest in Savage Club folklore was, at best, a mediocrity. Edwin Jehosophat Odell – for that was his improbable name – was a second-rate character actor who could barely have been called a gentleman, and who certainly was not, in the conventional sense, a good clubman. He was, however, a fine example of that legendary breed of clubmen: the club eccentric. "Old Odell" is commemorated at the Savage in oils and in marble, but his memory lives on most vividly in the chair from which he presided over club affairs for more than forty years. It is not the most famous chair in Clubland – the Athenaeum has Faraday's wheelchair and a chair of Charles Dickens, the Carlton displays Disraeli's chair from the Congress of Berlin, the Travellers' was given Thackeray's celebrated "cane bottom'd chair", and the Garrick has the seat on which Henry Irving died. It is, though, perhaps the most *infamous* chair in Clubland.

A history of the Savage Club written in 1907, when Odell was still alive, notes that he was "a man of uncertain age. He has been entertained to dinner on his seventieth, his eightieth, and his '1904th' birthdays. All these birthdays were comprised within ten years, and the seventieth came only the other day." Older members remembered seeing Odell on stage as Polonius, and (appropriately) as Gaspard the Miser in *Les cloches de Corneville*. He had a minor role in fellow Savage W.S. Gilbert's *Dan'l Druce*. Gilbert's verdict on this performance was terse: "Odell is simply damnable." Another Savage concluded that by the 1880s Odell had "long since decided that instead of continuing his career as a struggling character actor, he would concentrate on playing one role only – that of Odell, the uncrowned King of Bohemia." It is no wonder that he took refuge in the Savage; it was the only place that would put up with him.

Odell was a constant thorn in the side of the Savage Club committee. In July 1896 a special meeting was called to consider Odell's indebtedness for food and bedrooms. Ten years previously he had been disciplined for striking a servant. He was expelled at one point for publicly recommending candidates join another club, but was saved by the petitions of fifty members. Odell held all rules and authority figures in contempt. He barely spent a penny of his own money but would rather sit in his chair close to the bar, wearing his customary black sombrero and cloak, and scrounge Irish whiskey and cigars from his fellow members. (If offered a cigarette he would thunder, "I do not smoke stationary"). On one occasion Odell borrowed five pounds from a new member on his first visit to the club. After six months the young man asked whether he might be reimbursed. "I haven't finished with it yet", came the reply.

His fellow Savages regarded Odell as a pillar of the club, a totem of the Savage spirit, and backed him against his foes at every turn. Eventually reduced to penury, the ever patient Savages petitioned King Edward VII (a Brother Savage) to exercise his right to nominate Odell as a Poor Brother of the Charterhouse. The Royal Savage agreed, and Odell moved into the Charterhouse in 1908, where he remained for the next two decades.

Odell's greatest performance came in 1928, when he repaid the late king's generosity by behaving atrociously to one of his relatives. In this year HRH the Duke of York attended a merrification at which he was elected an honorary life member. The duke was treated to a typical programme of entertainments, including a Shakespearian soliloquy by Odell. After his performance the vain old actor left to find a drink elsewhere, refusing to watch any of the other turns. He returned to the Savage around 11pm. Thrusting his way cantankerously through the revellers, Odell headed towards his customary chair, only to find that it was occupied by the newly elected Royal Savage. A member recorded what happened next. "Livid with rage and waving his arms wildly, he shouted, 'Out of my chair, sir! Get out! – AT ONCE!' The duke obliged, removing himself apologetically to the bar, making the customary throne available to the obviously eccentric patriarch." This was to be Odell's last great show; he died four months later.

After the old devil had been buried, his brother Savages affixed to that same chair a plaque in his memory. It states plainly but affectionately the facts of the matter: "Here Old Odell Sat". In all their subsequent moves the chair has followed the Savages and remains amongst their most treasured possessions. It stands as a reminder that in Clubland, sheer pig-headed longevity counts for more than birth, titles, manners, or money. Let this be a cautionary tale for any royal dukes who might be reading.

28

THE FARMERS CLUB

IMPROVED ESSEX PIG

Every London club has its country members, those gentlemen who arrive into the metropolis wide-eyed and brown-shoed, ready to give in to all the temptations of the Big City. For the Farmers Club the standard ratio is reversed, with fully 95% of its members living outside of London. This should not come as a surprise, for whilst urban farming does apparently exist in places like Shoreditch, it bares as much resemblance to actual farming as quinoa does to actual food. The great majority of members are *bona fide* farmers, with the remainder gathered from ancillary trades. Because of this critical link to the farming profession, the Farmers Club is not so much a place of leisure as a leisurely space in which to conduct business. A barman in the 1960s remarked that "Members drink more when they grumble and some of them grumble a lot. But when the Common Market idea fell through, they drank quite a lot more to celebrate." One suspects that there has been a great deal more grumbling, and therefore a great more drinking, over the last sixty years, which have been as tumultuous a time for Britain's farmers as any point in the nation's history. Just listen to *The Archers*.

The club was founded in 1842 to promote in London the interests of those who dwelt in the countryside, and to provide a venue for farmers to discuss their trade. To a significant extent, this is still the role that the club plays today. Members gather to hear papers on agricultural machinery and crop strains, or to attend talks from the minister for farming and the environment. Trips are arranged each year to visit the nation's great agricultural shows. Not exactly everyone's cup of tea, but then the Farmers Club is not there to appeal to everyone. On a more populist note, the Farmers' clubhouse has a smashing balcony looking out onto the Thames, and the club is always rammed for the fireworks on New Year's Eve.

The clubhouse is smart, chic even, not at all what one might reasonably expect from a club with such a rustic dedication. Whilst there is no single object of great value or exceptional beauty that leaps out to the visitor, no city-slicker can fail to be charmed by the bucolic scenes hanging on the walls. Particularly pleasing are the pictures of prize animals from the great days of selective breeding. These include the famous "Durham Ox", whose weight at his peak was estimated at somewhere between 171 and 270 stone. Whilst there is something quite intimidating about a giant cow, immensely fat pigs are an enduring source of comfort. I suppose it reminds one of Wodehouse's *Blandings* novels, and just think of all that bacon. Of all the new pig breeds introduced around the dawn of the nineteenth century, the "Improved Essex Pig" is the jolliest, and has the most amusing name.

The landowner and Whig politician Charles Western was touring Italy when he took a fancy to some Neapolitan pigs. "Aha!" thought Western with admirable perspicacity, "these are just what I need to bulk-up my puny porkers back in Essex." Western procured a pair of Neapolitan boars which he took back to his estate and introduced to his sows. It was then left to one of Western's tenants to do the hard work. Mr Fisher Hobbs of Boxted Lodge (which sounds like the start to a dirty ditty) crossed the Neapolitan-Essex boars belonging to Lord Western with his own coarse Essex sows, establishing what came to be known as the Improved Essex. In 1840, Hobbs entered a boar and a sow from the new breed into the second show of the Royal Agricultural Society at Cambridge, and both obtained the first prize in their respective classes. The pigs gained a national reputation and quickly became one of the most prized breeds amongst British farmers. Fisher Hobbs, that intrepid pig-breeder of intriguing name, was also one of the founders of the Farmers Club, serving on its executive committee until his demise in 1866.

The "Old Essex", as the primitive breed was known retrospectively, had been a smallish, coarse, black and white animal, easily managed and cheap to feed. The Improved Essex retained the distinctive colouring and hardy character of its ancestor, but was capable of being bred to a much greater size. During the Second World War the Improved Essex had a resurgence in popularity because of the animals' ability to feed themselves through foraging. Pig for Victory! Shortly thereafter, however, numbers fell into a steep decline as British farmers were encouraged to forgo local variety and to focus on three staple breeds: the Welsh, the Landrace, and the Large White, in order to remain internationally competitive. Such is the banality of modernity.

In 1967 the Essex pig technically ceased to exist when the breed was merged with the neighbouring Wessex variety to become the British Saddleback. Today numbers of even this variety are declared to be "at risk" by the British Pig Association.[56] *Sic transit porcus mundi.* Some optimists believe that there are still a tiny number of purebreds maintained by covert enthusiasts, but this is probably wishful thinking. Short of some sort of porcine Jurassic Park scenario we must accept that the Improved Essex Pig has snuffled off to the great pigsty in the sky.[57] In one place at least the memory of the breed is kept alive. In the heart of Westminster, far from any farms, in the club which Fisher Hobbs helped to found, the breed peers down beadily from the walls as gentlemen farmers from across Britain tuck into their sausages.

---

[56] The British Pig Association sounds like a lot of fun. I wonder, does one has to be a pig to join, or do they accept fellow travellers?
[57] Jurassic Pork? I'd watch it.

29

THE LONDON SKETCH CLUB

SILHOUETTE FRIEZE

Clubland has a fractious streak, and several surviving clubs originated as splinter cells formed after a disagreement. This propensity towards schism is especially pronounced in North American clubs, owing to the independent temperament of the American people: "don't tread on me" etc. Whilst the fracture lines in North America have tended to be moral – slavery and civil rights – it is hard to imagine a disagreement more petty than that which led to the birth of the London Sketch Club.

In the second half of the nineteenth century, sketch artists were in great demand to fill the pages of illustrated papers such as *Punch* and *The Graphic*. Many of these artists met at the Langham Sketch Club (Est. 1838), where each Friday evening they would gather to practice their art, critically appraise each other's work, and share gossip. These gatherings were followed by a slap-up supper of bread and cheese. In 1898 an argument broke out between members who wanted to have a heartier hot supper, and those who resented any change to the established pattern. The *contretemps* between the hot and cold factions became so disagreeable that several members broke away and formed the London Sketch Club. For sensitive readers I am pleased to report that this story has a happy-ish ending. Although they remain two separate clubs, a German bomb forced a friendly truce between the parties. With the Langham's premises having been destroyed, their members now meet at the London Sketch Club. Their work is followed, of course, by a cold supper.

In 1957 the Sketch Club moved to Chelsea, selling its former premises on Marylebone Road to Woolworths; an upsetting fate, but one which funded a great many hot suppers.[58] Alongside the prints and sketches that one would expect, there are a number of interesting trophies collected over the years. These include a full-size street lamp wrenched from London Bridge during a drunken spree, and an eighteenth century cell door liberated from Newgate Prison. The latter opens to reveal a solid wall and a copy of Gustave Doré's sketch of Newgate Prison exercise yard. A jolly little barroom, dubbed The Sketchers' Arms, doubles-up as a changing room for life drawing models. Above the bar are displayed a range of fearsome looking weapons, which on closer inspection are revealed to be theatrical props. So life-like are these objects that their creator, the stained glass designer George Parlby, was arrested whilst carting them home and had to be rescued from prison by an embarrassed daughter.

Life in most clubs revolves around the bar or the coffee room, but the studio is the true soul of the London Sketch Club. This light and lofty room contains the

---

[58] The Dilke Street clubhouse forms part of "The Knowledge" which black cab drivers are required to memorise, owing to the great number of fancy dress parties held at the premises.

club's most extraordinary feature: a silhouette frieze of notable members, living and deceased. The tradition of silhouetting members began early in the club's history as a way of commemorating its leading artists, artistically. Sketch artists are not the pop stars they once were, and today most of the names are recognisable only to the initiated and the obsessive. However, there are several whose fame lives on in their work.

Tom Browne, a founder member of the Sketch Club, is silhouetted with a cigarette clamped between his teeth. Browne created the strutting dandy still used on bottles of *Johnnie Walker* whisky. Phil May was a prodigious drinker, noted horseman, and is considered to be the father of the modern cartoon. In silhouette one cannot see the phosphorescent rosiness of his substantial nose. May appears to be poking John Hassall in the chest. So prolific was Hassall's output that he was known as "The Poster King" of Edwardian England. Hassall's famous 1908 poster "Skegness is so bracing" is still being employed by Skegness Council over 110 years later. (It also inspired *Viz Comic*'s typically subtle homage: "Skegness is fucking shit"). Despite his commercial success, Hassell took a make-do-and-mend mentality to eccentric levels. He would patch-up old copper kettles with brown paper rather than throw them away, believing that all kettles developed their own personalities, and to dispose of them would hurt their feelings. Hassall designed the cover of *Scouting For Boys* for fellow member Robert Baden-Powell, who in addition to being the hero of Mafeking and the founder of the Boy Scouts was a talented ambidextrous sketcher.

Amiable oddball W. Heath Robinson is one of the few sketch artists of the inter-war generation whose work continues to appeal to a wide audience, owing principally to his cartoons of whimsically elaborate contraptions. Robinson became president of the Sketch Club in 1920, a post always held for a single year. Several of his family members followed W. Health into the club, so he is one of several Robinsons immortalised in the frieze.

These days the membership of the London Sketch Club includes more laymen than it does professional sketch artists, but the studio remains a place of work. Here artists may lift up their eyes – and possibly their hearts – to the rafters, and seek inspiration from the great men who have come before them. And when they have done so they can have a good hot supper and be thankful that it is the London Sketch Club and not the Langham which was spared the Luftwaffe's bomb.

30

CHELSEA ARTS CLUB

JAMES MCNEILL WHISTLER BY ALFRED THOMPSON

The Chelsea Arts Club exists on the edge of London's Clubland, both literally and euphemistically. Literally because it is on Old Church Street. Euphemistically because it occupies a liminal space between respectability and bohemianism shared perhaps only by Blacks Club in Soho. There are other arty London clubs – the Garrick or the Savile for example – but these are more stolidly *clubby*, requiring jackets, and discouraging beat poetry circles after lunch. At one point the Chelsea Arts Club was comparably genteel, but in recent decades all caution has been thrown into the appropriately coloured recycling bin, and an avant-gardist posture has been struck. The result is gloriously chaotic. In few clubs, anywhere in the world, will you meet such a selection of people. Outrageous homosexuals in lurid trousers exchange witticisms with resentful, wealthy directors of unwatchable one-woman shows. It is one of the few worthwhile places to have a drink in London where one can be quite certain that financiers are outnumbered by flautists.

The bar is the club's throbbing, libidinous core. On a Saturday night it is packed with all manner of exotic creatures, swaying along to some musical entertainment, or lamenting the prudishness of the nation's youth. The walls of the bar feature an eclectic and rotating assortment of art produced by members of the club, living, barely living, and dead. These works are sometimes poorly conceived and overtly pornographic, but there are always a few gems.

A charming feature of the Chelsea Arts Club is its garden, which is heavenly in the summer. For reasons best left unasked, the committee decided to replace the lawn with synthetic Astroturf. Perhaps it is an interactive art installation, cocking a snook at the passé notion of mortality. For if, as the prophet says, all flesh is as grass, at the CAC at least that grass withereth not, but like the word of the Lord it endureth forever.

The dining room is much more typical of Clubland, serving modern cuisine in an Edwardian setting. The art here is less experimental, presumably to ensure that diners are not given indigestion. A painting of particular interest, both for its subject and its artist, is a portrait of James McNeill Whistler by Alfred "Tommy" Thompson, which hangs against the back wall. Whistler, one of the greatest portraitists of his day, is identified by his expertly tousled mop, Cavalier facial hair, and monocle. Whistler's lean face scrutinises his viewers with a dandyish insouciance.

A wag once observed that Whistler is best known as the man with the fourth most famous mother in history, after Jesus Christ, Oedipus, and Principal Skinner from *The Simpsons*. Yet the artist was no mummy's boy. Originally destined for a career in the military, Whistler's inattentiveness in class (a roommate described him as "one of the most indolent of mortals") led to his being booted out of West Point Military Academy by the superintendent and future Confederate General, Robert E. Lee. Pursuing instead his interest in painting, Whistler remained pugnacious into old age. Ruskin, Swinburne and Wilde were the most famous victims of Whistler's acid tongue and litigious temperament. On another occasion the artist broke his hand assaulting a fellow passenger on-board a river steamer, braying that "the black scoundrel deserved his kicking". Whistler's magnificent society portraits channel this combative energy, giving his work a swashbuckling quality that lifts him above more staid contemporaries.

During the course of a career that was successfully transatlantic, Whistler came to call London his home.

Here he was instrumental in founding the Chelsea Arts Club. Chelsea in the later nineteenth century was awash with artists, and it was only natural that they should seek to club together for their mutual benefit. Under Whistler's leadership the club emerged as a rival to the older and more respectable Arts Club in Mayfair. A property was acquired in 1891 and furnished hastily and economically, but not without taste.

Whistler's likeness is captured by Alfred Thompson, a fascinating gentleman and accomplished artist in his own right; and of course a member of the Chelsea Arts Club. Thompson was deaf from birth, and although he briefly attended art school he was largely self-taught. These impediments did not stop Thompson becoming an official artist with the RAF during the Second World War. His portrait of the club's most illustrious founder member is based on an etching by Paul Cesar Helleu, drawn from life in 1897. (Helleu is better known for his many beautiful paintings of many beautiful women, as well as for conceiving the mural of stellar constellations on the ceiling of New York's Grand Central Terminal.) In this painting, Thompson has taken the liberty of placing Whistler's monocle on the correct eye, although it is reversed in Helleu's etching.

One more thing about Thompson is worth noting: he was the final Olympian to win a gold medal for painting. Art competitions of various sorts were part of the Olympic programme from 1912 until the London Olympics of 1948, at which Thompson won his gold medal for a painting entitled "The London Amateur Boxing Championship". The inclusion of artistic disciplines alongside feats of sporting prowess was regarded by the movement's founding fathers as integral to the Olympic spirit, reflecting the place that art had alongside sport in the ancient Athenian games. Medals were awarded in such disciplines as Compositions for Orchestra, Town Planning, Lyric and Speculative Works (in the field of Literature), and Mixed Sculpturing. These artistic competitions were dropped from the Olympic programme in 1952, due (supposedly) to logistical constraints, although one suspects it was simply the result of rampant philistinism. Lamentable though one may find the demise of Olympic art, it gives a special place to dear deaf Alfred Thompson, one of the true heroes of the Chelsea Arts Club, and a *bona fide* gold medal painter.

SECTION TWO

PROVINCIAL CLUBS

31

THE FREWEN CLUB (OXFORD)

MR PUNCH BOWL

Oxford is a clubbable city. The common rooms, bars, and butteries of its ancient university are pullulating with bright young things seeking distraction from their studies. Indeed it was probably in Oxford that the term "club" was first applied, however loosely, to those who met at the coffee house opened by Arthur Tillyard
218

in 1655. The Oxford Coffee Club was comprised of both students and fellows who would meet to discuss the latest scientific theories and to share the fruits of their research. Their number included Sir Robert Boyle, that distinguished and pious chemist. This Oxford Coffee Club was eventually to evolve into the Royal Society, proving once again that a clubbable spirit can change the world for the better.

Not all of the clubs formed amidst the Dreaming Spires have contributed to the total sum of human knowledge. The Dangerous Sports Club, created in Oxford in the late 1970s, might well have cancelled out by its stupidity the achievements of the Oxford Coffee Club. Always more of a loose assemblage of eccentrics than a club in the developed sense, its stunts included holding a Black Tie High Tea on the perilously uninhabitable island of Rockall, pioneering the pseudo-sport of surrealist skiing at St Moritz, and inventing the bungee jump. In 2002 the Dangerous Sports Club accidentally killed a student by firing him from a trebuchet. Oops.[59]

---

[59] David Kirke, the founder of the Dangerous Sports Club, might still be found in the King's Arms on Holywell Street. He will share stories of the club with anyone who is willing to listen.

The Frewen Club is an altogether more conservative beast than either of the above. It was formed in 1869 by the officers and NCOs of the 2nd Oxfordshire Rifle Volunteer Corps, and was initially called the 2nd Oxfordshire Rifle Volunteer Corps Club, an honest if unimaginative name. The club settled at its current location on the strict understanding with the landlord that there was to be "no spitting out of the window into the street". It was renamed the Frewen Club in 1888 and membership was opened to Oxford residents. Like Japanese knotweed or the American grey squirrel, the civilians gradually drove out any military types and assumed full control of the club shortly thereafter.

Appealing as it does to the town rather than the gown, the Frewen remains blissfully unconcerned by radical student politics, which have infiltrated certain of the University's dining clubs, and consequently it is still lads only. Its membership consists principally of local businessmen and other hearty civic types who do not have SCRs in which to lunch.

Tucked away behind an unmarked emerald portal opposite Christ Church, the Frewen celebrated its sesquicentennial in 2019 by publishing a history of the club called *Behind the Green Door*, a title it shares with a genre-defining pornographic film released in 1972.[60] The Frewen's clubhouse is stoutly Yeomanic, all wood panelling, darts, and ale. In common with every club, the Frewen has its quirks. It is club practice for the retiring president to present a gift at the end of his term in office. One donation consisted of two military bugles. After a series of noise complaints, made within the first week of this generous bequest, and culminating in a police visit, the instruments were quietly disposed of. The sitting president is reserved a throne-like chair adjacent to the bar, and if another member presumes to occupy this seat when the president is in residence then club tradition dictates that he must buy everyone present a round of drinks. Mine's a quadruple scotch with Bollinger chaser!

The Frewen has a proud sporting tradition, particularly in the disciplines of golf, snooker, darts, and conkers. Take it from me that when one has witnessed a dozen heavily refreshed pensioners energetically thwacking each other's knuckles with conkers then it is not a sight which is soon forgotten. Trophies are awarded in each of these disciplines and

---

[60] With thanks to the Rev'd Yaroslav Walker for this observation.

there is a fine array of silverware displayed behind the bar.

Amongst this collection one piece stands out for its handsome appearance and ridiculous history. This is a punch bowl of generous dimensions, inscribed with the names and dates of the Frewen's presidents. The bowl was purchased in 1926 following a general appeal. There has been an annual Punch Night at the Frewen since 1886 and to this day there is an appointed club brewer entrusted with the secret recipe for Frewen Punch. Taking place close to Christmas it is a welcome excuse for festive rowdiness; as if any excuse were needed.

A general meeting was called on the night that the punch bowl was presented to the club, marking the fortieth anniversary of Punch Night. The gathered members took it upon themselves to test the new bowl's suitability for its sacred charge. *Non nobis solum nati sumus* and all that. The capacious vessel was duly filled with the Frewen's legendarily potent punch. Having drunk deep and often, one highly lubricated member decided to propose the punch bowl for membership of the club. As everyone agreed that it was a very splendid punch bowl indeed the motion was passed unanimously. With all the wit that the membership could muster, the vessel was entered into the list of members as Mr Punch Bowl. As the motion has never been rescinded Mr Punch Bowl has the honour of being the oldest member of the Frewen Club, approaching the centennial of his distinguished tenure. Silly, silly, silly.

32

THE NOTTINGHAM CLUB

MARSHAL TALLART PLAQUE

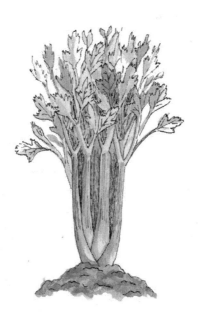

If Nottingham is known as "the Queen of the Midlands" (a coveted title in Birmingham's Theatre District) then the Nottingham Club is one of the jewels in its crown. The seventeenth century clubhouse is an oasis of civility in the midst of a brutalised city centre. The Nottingham and Nottinghamshire United Services Club, to use its full title, is a relative newcomer to Clubland, having only been incorporated in 1921. Lieutenant General Sir Brian Horrocks "regarded the forward edge of the battlefield as the most exclusive club in the world." It was in this spirit that the Nottingham Club was founded to further the comradeship developed on the battlefields of the Great War.

An Armistice Dinner remains the largest event in the club's social calendar, but it is another regular culinary event which has whetted our appetite. This is the annual Celery Lunch, in which – *quelle surprise* – each course is based around the delicately flavoured superfood. The source of this tradition is revealed in a plaque displayed on the clubhouse at 64 Castle Gate. It declares that the building, known as Newdigate House, was once the residence of the renowned Camille d'Hostun, duc de Tallard. Tallard was held as a prisoner of war in Nottingham following his capture at the Battle of Blenheim. The plaque misspells the Marshal's surname as Tallart, but at least they have managed the correct dates: 1705-1711.

Tallard's seven years in Nottingham were far from miserable. Daniel Defoe visited the former French military commander and declared his residence to be "small, but beautiful", decorated elegantly in the

French style. During his stay, the charming Tallard had no problem ingratiating himself with the local population. The Marshal's popularity with Nottingham's womenfolk was legendary; even today one can detect a certain Gallic quality amongst the city's residents. A typical Frenchman, the Marshal's greatest gift to the people of Nottingham was gastronomic. Tallard missed the food of his home country and was overjoyed when he spotted celery growing in the marshes of Lenton. He began to cultivate the plant, which was dismissed by the locals as a tasteless weed. Properly prepared, and no doubt given a certain social caché by its cultivator, the fibrous foodstuff became a Nottingham favourite. When the Marshal returned to France in 1711, the townsfolk continued to cultivate the celery plant in his memory.

The Nottingham Club's former premises were demolished in the 1960s along with much of the city centre to make way for the ugly and dispiriting Maid Marian Way. This act of vandalism turned out to be something of a blessing for Nottingham's clubmen, however, as the club relocated to Newdigate House, and so assumed the legacy of Marshal Tallard. Today the club has a Tallard Room and a Blenheim Room, along with a portrait of the house's former resident. Each year the membership gather for their Celery Lunch around the date of the Battle of Blenheim, wearing sticks of celery in their buttonholes and offering toasts to "The Marshal". A tasteful tribute to Nottingham's favourite adopted son.

33

THE NORFOLK CLUB (NORWICH)

BALLOT BOXES

If you are looking for an excuse to break open the carbonated grape juice then remember that in 2020 the Norfolk Club celebrates its 250th anniversary. This makes it the oldest club outside of London, and one of the most venerable in Britain. The Norfolk began its life as an aristocratic dining club, one of many which sprang up across the Anglosphere in that zealously clubbable age. On the 9th June 1770 a group of gentlemen:

> most sanguinely moved and proposed as
> follows: That a Select Number of intimate
> Friends in the County of Norfolk (not

exceeding fourteen) do dine together at the Bell Tavern in the Market Place Norwich upon the last Saturday in the months of June, July, August 1770 and in the months of April, May, June, July and August in the next ensuing year for ten years to come.

The document on which these words are inscribed is seven years older than the American Declaration of Independence, and most right-thinking persons would argue that it is of greater historical value, at least to the clubmen of Norwich. It has been framed and now hangs in the club's library. This dining club eventually expanded beyond its self-imposed and seemingly arbitrary limit of fourteen persons (twelve or thirteen would at least have been biblical), whilst retaining its aristocratic flavour. It took another one hundred and seventeen years before the Norfolk Club purchased its own premises at 17 Upper King Street; a smart eighteenth century mansion roughly contemporary with the club's founding, and which the club continues to call home today.

17 Upper King Street retains its traditional ambience whilst having adapted to modern standards of

comfort. In this way the club reflects the spirit of Norwich; a handsome medieval city less ravaged by Nazi bombs and the barbarisms of post-war town planners than many comparable metropoles. The clubhouse's décor and furnishings are precisely what one would expect: open fires, chesterfield armchairs, and pictures of racehorses owned by previous members. As befits a club at the heart of Nelson's county, an annual Trafalgar Day dinner crowns the social calendar.

The club has a couple of interesting features. A mosaic of Venetian tiles brightens up the hallway, and the portraits of royal patrons and notable alumni give some impression of the club's pedigree. Not unique to the Norfolk Club, but retained here in splendid array, are five of the balloting boxes which at one stage were a ubiquitous – and not uncontroversial – feature of Clubland.

Clubs are, by their very nature, exclusive. A club which will admit without prejudice ceases to be a club in any meaningful sense.[61] Until the recent past most clubs divided the clubbable wheat from the boorish chaff through an exercise in direct democracy, utilising

---

[61] One wag has called this "the freedom of disassociation".

precisely the sort of balloting boxes found in the Norfolk Club. The process was perfect in its simplicity. When presented with a candidate, existing members would vote by placing a ball into the box, and depositing it either in the side marked "Aye" or that marked "No". In many of the clubs which employed this system, a single "No" vote was enough to exclude that candidate from membership.

Some clubs utilised a system of white and black balls, with the black ball signifying a vote in the negative. Like so much that is laudable – such as naked wrestling and stuffed vine leaves – this is an invention of the ancient Greeks. For the citizens of Athens, a shard of black pottery in a voting box meant banishment; the fragments came from tiles known as ὄστρακα, from which we derive our word ostracism and the idea of "blackballing".

The history of Clubland is littered with the bodies of the blackballed, including those of some eminently clubbable men. Henry Irving was, on his first attempt, blackballed from the Garrick. Benjamin Disraeli was blackballed from White's. The doors to the Travellers were barred to Cecil Rhodes, Lord Rosebery, Lord Randolph Churchill, and W.M. Thackeray, the latter by a man who said, "We don't want any writing fellows here."

In the 1830s there was an epidemic of blackballing. White's was so reduced by this vindictive tit for tat "pilling" that it was forced to remove the rule about a single black ball being enough to exclude a candidate. Without this change White's was in danger resembling the Duke of Dorset's Junta Club in Max Beerbohm's *Zuleika Dobson*, the total membership of which was reduced to only three gentlemen, two of whom the duke regretted lowering his standards to admit.

Perhaps the greatest of Clubland's blackballing anecdotes took place in the 1780s. An aristocratic Irishman named George Robert FitzGerald was determined to join Brooks's, and bullied an acquaintance into putting him up for membership. However, "Fighting FitzGerald" had an unsavoury reputation. A man of many eccentricities, FitzGerald was in the habit of keeping wild bears as pets, hunting by moonlight, and duelling with anyone whom he disliked. Fighting FitzGerald took a dislike to a great many people. He killed his first man at the age of 16, whilst still at Eton. A few years later FitzGerald was shot in the head during another duel but recovered after an emergency trepanning. This incident did little to stabilise an already unbalanced temperament.

The insane Irishman insisted on waiting downstairs at Brooks's whilst his name was considered. When the ballot boxes were emptied, they were found to contain not a single white ball. Worried about FitzGerald's reaction, it was decided best to tell him that only one black ball had been cast, this being enough to exclude him. The white lie did not have the desired effect. When FitzGerald heard the news he declared: "I'm chose; but there must be a small matter of mistake in my election," and he persuaded a second vote.

This time he was told two black balls were thrown. "'Then," exclaimed Fitzgerald, "there's now two mistakes instead of one," and he persuaded a third vote. Finally he was told the truth, that all the balls thrown were black. FitzGerald stormed upstairs and asked each member face-to-face if he had thrown a black ball. Of course everyone denied that they had, whereupon FitzGerald addressed the whole body: "You see, Gentlemen, that as none of ye have black-balled me, I must be chose." He never set foot in Brooks's again, but everywhere told people that he had been duly elected as a member.

Two centuries after FitzGerald's irregular election to Brooks's, the ballot boxes at the Norfolk Club were put to use for the final time. In 1987 a husband and a wife were both up for membership. The boxes were passed around and the wife was admitted without a single objection. The husband, however, had one black ball thrown against him. There was then time for discussion, with the opportunity for the anonymous blackballer to change his or her mind. When the ballot box was passed around a second time the husband had received three black balls. The event caused such acrimony that the venerable boxes were retired from use, just one year shy of the club's centenary at 17 Upper King Street.

Today most clubs have dispensed with their balloting boxes in favour of a less potentially embarrassing means of vetting new members. For those of us who are already "in" this may be some cause for sadness. As a breed, clubmen are suspicious of change, favouring the customs and attitudes of a bygone age: when collars were starched, champagne came in pint bottles, and terrifying Irish noblemen threatened to murder those who stood in their way.

34

THE CARDIFF AND COUNTY CLUB

KYFFIN WILLIAMS SKETCH

The Cardiff and County Club is the only true outpost of Clubland to the west of Offa's Dyke. It stands as a beacon of old-fashioned civility in the Welsh capital; a city which has been modernised rapidly and inelegantly in recent decades. Founded in 1866 for shipping magnates and coal

owners, the club has occupied its current premises in the city centre since 1892. When it opened, the club's ostentatious Renaissance-inspired clubhouse was one of the most notable buildings in Cardiff. Today it is dwarfed by the vast bulk of the Millennium Stadium, which squats obstreperously opposite. Standing on the club's charming, rather whimsical balcony, or gazing out from the dining room, the stadium entirely fills the vista. It feels rather like sitting in a rowing boat whilst the Titanic passes by.

The interior of the clubhouse is masculine with playful touches; just the way I like 'em. The bar is furnished with handsome art deco armchairs in British Racing Green, which have the added benefit of being genuinely cosy. The dining room is cheerful and well used, and the club is graced with a dedicated staff who know what the members like. Pleasingly, the County Club still has a barber who comes and sets-up shop in the gentlemen's washroom on appointment. This practice used to be common in Clubland but today – like the older members' hair – it has all but vanished.[62]

There are a few interesting knick-knacks on display. The taxidermied head of a moose (named Matthew, obviously) guards the entrance to the dining room. A model of *The Welsh City*, a fishing vessel built, confusingly, in Glasgow, adds some interest to the first floor landing.

---

[62] The barber's chair now in the Cardiff and County Club used to belong to a barber's shop in Cardiff. It is the same chair in which the actor, singer, and possible Nazi collaborator Maurice Chevalier used to sit on his occasional visits to Cardiff.

More notable is the burgeoning art collection which the club has accrued over recent years. Until the millennium the County Club displayed works on loan from the National Museum of Wales. However, a small number of persons at the museum were unhappy with the club's policy of only admitting men to membership, and withdrew the artwork as a punitive measure. Chastened and contrite, the club voted to admit women in 2014.[63] It also responded by developing an art collecting policy, seeking works that will beautify the clubhouse whilst paying homage to the club's setting, both in Cardiff and in Wales more widely.

A.N. Wilson, a writer capable of being as offensive as a ballistic missile, once opined in the *London Evening Standard* that "The Welsh are held in universal derision. They have never made any significant contribution to any branch of knowledge or culture. Choral singing, usually flat, seems to be their only artistic attainment. They have no architecture, no gastronomic tradition, and since the Middle Ages, no literature worthy of the name. Even their religion,

---

[63] The policy was not universally popular. One member turned up the vote wearing a dress as an act of protest. However, as he did not conform to the club's dress-code he was expelled and his protest vote went unregistered.

Calvinistic Methodism, is boring." Certain bits of this tirade are, admittedly, hard to dispute. Surely, not even the most militant member of Plaid Cymru would argue that the Welsh national cuisine of cheese on toast deserved its place in Europe's gastronomic pantheon. Artistically, however, we must plead the Cymric case. In the twentieth century Wales produced a mighty battalion of scribblers, sculptors, and daubers. The Welsh also do a cracking line in poet priests, if that is your sort of thing.[64]

Perhaps the most alluring of these artists was Sir Kyffin Williams, whose work is represented in the County Club by two quite distinct pictures. The first is an oil painting of Notre Dame Cathedral, on loan from Sir David Davies. The second is a small pen and wash sketch which hangs in a corner of the bar, where it is easily overlooked. It depicts a weather-beaten farmer, short, slightly stooped from his years of labour, with intelligent eyes and a grim, disapproving mouth. He wears the uniform of the farming folk of North Wales. The sketch was presented to the staff of the County Club by Roy Bohana, former music director of the Arts

---

[64] If it is not your sort of thing then frankly I despair of you.

Council of Wales, a body which Kyffin regarded with undisguised contempt.

Sir Kyffin Williams was, it is fair to say, a difficult man. He could be contrarian, populist, and peevish, though also witty, wise, and prophetic. Towards the end of his life, Kyffin was elevated to secular sainthood by the Welsh art establishment; his public utterances prefaced by those awful words: "national treasure". By the 1980s his work was so desirable that one yuppie was heard to quip that "success is a house in Pontcanna, a Volvo in the garage, and a Kyffin on the wall."

Kyffin claimed to "paint in Welsh". As a child, he was sent to Shrewsbury School as a boarder. Here Kyffin's Welsh accent was quickly beaten out of him. Kyffin never forgot or forgave this attack on his Welshness. After the abject misery of school, a brief stint of National Service was terminated upon the discovery that Kyffin suffered from epilepsy, a condition which he was proud to share with Pablo Picasso. The military doctor dismissed him with the following sound advice: "Williams, as you are in fact abnormal, I think it would be a good idea if you took up art."

During his sixty active years as a painter, Kyffin produced hundreds of landscapes, portraits, and sketches. In oils he painted quickly, even feverishly, often completing a painting in a single sitting. Early on he developed the technique of painting with a palette knife, giving his works a ridged, textured quality. His palette was usually subdued, producing brooding sea and mountainscapes full of melancholic beauty. Although trips to Florence and Patagonia led to some of his most interesting compositions, he always returned to the mountains of North Wales and their hardy farming folk, seeing therein the true heart of Wales.

Kyffin was a vocal critic of much contemporary art, decrying its lack of beauty and apparent skill. As such he has been compared unfavourably to a "sort of Nigel Farage of the art world, to whom the press could always turn for a provocative quote." The last laugh has been Kyffin's. In death he has become the doyen of the Welsh art establishment, whilst many of those faddish modernists whom he so reviled have fallen out of favour. His range may have been limited, but it was consistently arresting. Even the funny little pen and wash figure of the farmer propping up the bar at the Cardiff and County Club possesses a certain mournful dignity. A dignity, it must be said, quite at odds with some of the club's other denizens after a convivial and well lubricated lunch.

35

THE ATHENAEUM (LIVERPOOL)

WOOLLEN LAWS

Liverpool used to have several clubs, back before the world was old. The grandest was the Lyceum which opened its doors in 1802. The Lyceum's fate was sealed when the city centre was ravaged in the Blitz. Its glorious neo-classical clubhouse now stands empty, too big for the needs of the modern world. The Racquet Club, founded in 1877, had an equally dramatic demise; it was one of seventy buildings which burned down in the Toxteth Riots of 1981.

Today only two Scouse clubs survive. There is the Artists' Club, a plucky little survivor known to its members as the "Piss Artists", and then there is the Athenaeum.

Let's get one thing straight. The Liverpool Athenaeum is not some northern franchise of its more famous London namesake. Although both clubs have the same dedication, the Liverpool Ath' predates the London Ath' by almost thirty years. So you can stick that in your southern pipe for starters. We can probably thank the French for giving the Athenaeum its *raison d'être*. The club was founded during a period of phenomenal growth for Liverpool, in population, reputation, and wealth. This growth owed much to the seemingly endless round of French wars with which the Georgians kept themselves busy (it is important to have a hobby.) As the most significant port on the western seaboard, Liverpool became a vital strategic and commercial centre. In 1797, the elders of Liverpool decided to build themselves a venue worthy of the city's new stature, where they might receive the latest news from the battlefields and trading routes on which their prosperity depended. To this day the social heart of the club is known as the news room. It contains a little bust of Napoleon, as a nod to his role in the club's foundation.

The founding fathers of the Athenaeum did not stop here. Their club was to be more than a place to discuss profit margins and sales figures. It was to house a splendid library, one of the first – and finest – club libraries in Europe. As well as maps, globes, and navigation charts, the library contained all that was necessary for a classic liberal education. Hence the club's dedication to Athena, goddess of wisdom and war. When the Athenaeum moved to its current premises in 1924, the news room and the library were reconstructed and they remain the club's twin foci. These rooms contain several fine portraits, mostly of local worthies, but also of a few more nationally recognisable faces. On the staircase there are portraits of every prime minister from Pitt the Younger to Churchill, but none thereafter. Perhaps this is a matter of limited space, or it may be a commentary on declining prime ministerial standards. The club's literary relics include a signed volume of Florence Nightingale's *Notes on Hospitals*, a hand written 1449 translation of Cicero's *Orations*, and a copy of *Magna Carta* from 1282.

In the midst of all of these treasures, one can be forgiven for missing the barely legible scrap of paper which is hidden above the librarian's desk in a corner of an otherwise unremarkable office. It was given to the Athenaeum by Liverpool parish church, whose clergy played a role in the club's foundation, and attests to one of the stranger and more unpopular episodes in English legal history. This is a legal document from the seventeenth century, which swears that the corpse of the late Joseph Benson "was not put in, wrapt or wound up, in any shirt, shift, shoot or shroud, made or mingled with flax, silk, hair, gold or silver". Well done Joe Benson, one might say, but why should we care? This remarkable oath derives from what one Victorian commentator called "an absurd and vexatious Act of Parliament" passed in 1666, which legislated that only woollen shrouds be used for interring the dead. If an individual was found to have infringed this law then there would be imposed a fine of £5 – no meagre sum – which would be given half to the informer and half to the poor of the parish.

What, then, was the purpose of this arcane piece of legislation? In the high Middle Ages wool was the principal source of England's wealth. Witness the great woollen churches of the Cotswolds and East

Anglia, built with the profits from a booming continental woollen trade. Fashions changed as they always do, and in the sixteenth century linen, satin, and silk became more readily available, and the demand for woollen cloth fell away. With the industry in decline, creative measures were needed to increase demand. Members of Parliament whose constituencies were affected by the decline collaborated to pass the Act for Burying in Woollen. Their stated objectives were "lessening the importation of linen from beyond the seas, and the encouragement of the woollen and paper manufacturers of the kingdom."

From the beginning the law was hard to enforce, and widely unpopular. Many wished to bury their dead in the finest materials they could afford, not to dump them in the ground in a woollen sack. Others were less concerned; after all, what did clothes matter in the afterlife? In 1731, Alexander Pope composed a verse which mocked the vanity of those who opposed the law:

Odious! in woollen! 'twould a saint provoke!

(Were the last words that poor Narcissa spoke).

No! let a charming chintz and Brussels lace

Wrap my cold limbs, and shade my lifeless face

The law was repealed in 1814, but it had fallen out of use several decades previously. The affidavit which is preserved in the Athenaeum is a rarity, since most like it have been lost or destroyed. This may not be the most beautiful treasure in the Athenaeum, but it does serve as a reminder that no industry retains its vigour forever. Like the woollen trade before it, the shipping industry which made Liverpool so wealthy in the eighteenth and nineteenth centuries is long gone. Yet after years in the doldrums[65] Liverpool is booming once more, buoyed up by hospitality and tourism. Through prosperity and poverty, revelry and riot, falling bombs and failing industries, the Liverpool Athenaeum has remained a constant presence in the city centre. In recent decades the club has acquired a further significance: it is perhaps the only place in the whole city – and this includes both of its cathedrals – where one can escape the omnipresent legacy of The Beatles.

---

[65] Or should that be doldra?

36

THE HARROGATE CLUB

SIR ARTHUR CONAN DOYLE'S BILLIARDS CUE

On a sunny day, if you squint a little, the market town of Harrogate feels like a chunk of Mayfair has been transplanted to North Yorkshire. The women are fashionable, the tourists pestilential, and the shops are *too, too chic.* It is only appropriate that Harrogate is graced by its own little outpost of Clubland – the Harrogate Club – founded in 1857, and located at "Harrogate's most prestigious address" on Victoria Avenue since 1886. The clubhouse is notable principally for its elegantly curved bay windows and handsome stonework. Past members have included the industrialist and llama breeder Sir Titus Salt; and Cuthbert Broderick, architect of Leeds' stupendous circular Corn Exchange.

Our object from the Harrogate Club is so unassuming that it was almost lost to posterity. This is Sir Arthur Conan Doyle's billiards cue, which was presented to the club by a relative of the author. The cue was gratefully received and placed beside the billiard table. A reasonable location for such a bequest one might think, but as the cue was not signed, and failed to proclaim its exalted pedigree by glowing with supernal light, Sir Arthur's cue was indistinguishable from the regular cues. The most likely candidate has now been identified, but as with those churches which claim to have St Boniface's larynx or the trouser-press of St Elmo, one ought to approach this literary relic with a *soupçon* of scepticism.

The creator of Sherlock Holmes was a frequent visitor to the Harrogate Club, and on these occasions he enjoyed playing billiards with the members. A contemporary at the club commended Conan Doyle for being in the "front rank of amateur players", describing him as a "dour opponent, smoking his pipe, concentrating intensely on every shot, reminding one of Sherlock Holmes in one of his contemplative moods." Sir Arthur's visit to the Harrogate Club in February 1920 was rather more serious than usual, as he addressed the membership on that weightiest of topics, "Is there life after death?" On this occasion Sir Arthur played his customary game of billiards, but he also delved into spookier territory, participating in a séance held to mark his visit.

Conan Doyle's interest in the supernatural was first piqued in 1889, when he attended a lecture on mesmerism given by Milo de Meyer. Despite the fact that de Meyer tried and failed to hypnotize Conan Doyle, the author's faith in the power of mesmerism was only strengthened. Five years later, Conan Doyle became convinced that he had witnessed a supernatural "uproar" at a house haunted by the spirit of a dead child.

From 1917 onwards, the author channelled his full energies into promoting the spiritualist cause, touring the country speaking on the power of séances, mediums, and visitations from beyond the grave. It was such an event which brought him to the Harrogate Club in the February of 1920. The irony did not escape Conan Doyle's many fans that the author's credulous belief in ghoulies was at odds with the extreme rationalism of his most famous literary creation. Sir Arthur's reputation took a further knock when he published *The Coming of the Fairies* in 1922, in which he promoted the existence of fairies on the basis of "photographic evidence" provided by two young girls from the Yorkshire village of Cottingley, twenty miles southwest of Harrogate.

Although Arthur Conan Doyle became a figure of ridicule to many, he was a hero in spiritualist circles. Within days of his death in 1930 a spiritualist meeting was held at the Royal Albert Hall, to offer Conan Doyle the chance to make his final farewells from beyond the grave. Ten thousand attended, but one chair was left empty in case the great man himself returned in spiritual form. As it happened, Sir Arthur chose not to disturb the gathering. This was probably for the best. As Margot Asquith once observed, "I always knew the living talked rot, but it is nothing to the nonsense the dead talk." In a wishy-washy Anglican sense, Conan Doyle does live on of course through his perennially popular stories. There are also rumours abroad in the Harrogate Club that on stormy nights, when the moon is full, one might witness a certain billiards cue being raised by spectral hands, ready to take a ghostly pot shot...

THE NEW CLUB (EDINBURGH)

ROBERT BARKER'S PANORAMA

In central Edinburgh, on an insalubrious stretch of road, stands the New Club. Edinburgh deserves the New Club and the New Club contains something of the spirit of Edinburgh. Which is to say that it is stately but rather severe, venerable yet modern, enlightened in spirit but Jacobite in sympathy, and soundly, profoundly charming. The New Club was the brainchild of James Cunningham, 14th Earl of Glencairn. Cunningham is better known as a patron of Rabbie Burns. If you are looking for someone to blame for enabling the Bard of Ayrshire's interminable Romantic ramblings then look no further than the 14th Earl of Glencairn. It was at the first Royal Caledonian Hunt Ball in 1787, held in Edinburgh's splendid new assembly rooms, that Cunningham proposed a "new club" for the menfolk of the city, which would reflect Edinburgh's growth into a centre of intellectual and economic activity that rivalled any of the great capitals of Europe.

The club at first lacked a permanent home, but a splendid classical clubhouse was eventually constructed on Princess Street. Things flourished in the second half of the nineteenth century, and thereafter remained fairly bonnie until the 1960s (a statement which holds true for Western civilisation more generally). By this point the building was crumbling and unsuited to the demands of the modern clubman. So the whole thing came down and a new clubhouse made of panels of granite and glass was constructed in its place. Looking at this building from the outside, this decision seems to be on a par with flared trousers and the escalation of the Vietnam War on the list of "bad things to come out of the 1960s". To the right is a tourist shop selling "Wee Jimmy" hats. To the left is a branch of Ann Summers, a lingerie retailer frequented by awkward teenage boys and middle-aged divorcees looking for affordable Valentine's Day gifts. The club's doorway is undistinguished almost to the point of invisibility.

Once entrance has been gained, however, the genius of the 1960s design becomes apparent. The principal rooms are spacious, and the furniture and pictures from the old clubhouse do not seem out of place – often an unfortunate consequence of moving to a new building. Large panel windows fill the building with light, and present spectacular views of the city's majestic skyline. The coffee room retains the original wood panelling, which is a nice touch. A favourite feature of the 1960s design is the inbuilt ashtrays above the urinals in the cloakroom.

Until recently those using the club were presented with two options when they reached the reception desk; left for gentlemen and right for ladies. This arrangement continued with mutual approval until the Scottish Parliament passed new equality legislation in 2010, after which the club "went fully bisexual", in the words of the secretary. A small distinction between the two halves is still retained: gentlemen are required to wear ties in the rooms to the left, but not in those to the right.

There are a few treasures worth noting. On the top floor there is a giant stone urn which once sat atop the old clubhouse. There had been nine but only one was retained for posterity. Another was taken by Sir Nicholas Fairbairn, the Scottish Tory, in exchange for a painting of his own composition. This was hardly a fair swap, and the unfortunate picture has been relegated to an out-of-the-way lavatory.

In the silence room on the first floor are a couple of chairs that appear to be ecclesiastical in design.[66] In fact these belong to a mysterious dining society called the Monks of St Giles. This Victorian foundation has nothing to do with the city's High Kirk, dedicated to St Giles, nor are they linked to any monastery. These monks are devoted to the discussion and composition of literature, and the pursuit of inebriation. One

---

[66] Now smoking is forbidden in the smoking room, is shouting encouraged in the silence room?

evening a few years ago the fire alarm sounded and the New Club was evacuated. Alongside the regular members there trooped out onto Princes Street several eminent gentlemen wearing flowing grey habits, hoods pulled up against the wind, or perhaps to shield them from the bemused looks of passers-by. Upon joining the Order, members are required to take a name in religion which is then recorded on their chair. One brass plaque reads "FABULUS". Well, quite.

Less flashy but more interesting is a copy of the original panorama, which hangs amongst the club's world class collection of prints and etchings. The panorama was the invention of Robert Barker, an itinerant Irish painter who moved to Edinburgh in the 1780s. This fortuitous relocation would result in his creating one of the most popular and lucrative entertainment forms of the age.

Barker supposedly hit upon his idea whilst trekking up Edinburgh's Calton Hill one rare sunny afternoon in 1787, the same year that the New Club was forming in the imagination of the 14th Earl of Glencairn. From Barker's vantage he could see the whole city laid out before him. Using some self-designed apparatus, the artist enlisted the help of his twelve-year-old son,

Henry, to sketch out a 360 degree view of Edinburgh. The result was something quite unique; a view of the city "in the round". That same year Barker patented the design for a circular building designed to confine the visitor's visual field in a way which fooled the eye into thinking that it was viewing reality rather than a canvas. Despite discouraging words from a sceptical Joshua Reynolds, Barker produced a larger version of his original image, formed into a circle measuring twenty-five feet in diameter. The guard room of Holyrood Palace served as his studio. The age of panoromania had begun.

Panorama is a union of the Greek words Πάν meaning "all" and ὅραμα meaning "that which is seen". It was the "brunch" of its day, insofar as it was both a *portmanteau* and instantly, faddishly popular. Barker took his design to London and here made his fortune. Even Sir Joshua Reynolds was contrite, admitting "I find I was in error in supposing your invention could never succeed, for the present exhibition proves it is capable of producing effects, and representing nature in a manner superior to the limited scale of pictures in general." Like modern economic theory, philosophical empiricism, and the deep-fried Mars Bar, the panorama is Scotland's gift to the world. It is a manifestation of the same Enlightenment spirit which shaped Edinburgh's glorious New Club in that city's golden age.

THE GLASGOW ARTS CLUB

CHARLES RENNIE MACKINTOSH FINGER PLATES

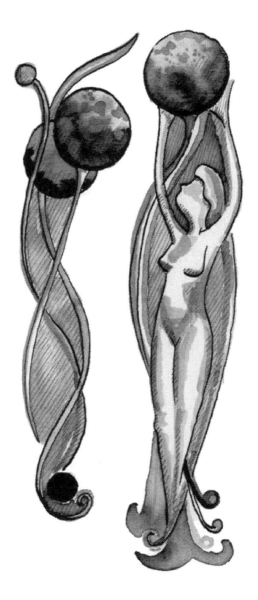

The Glasgow Arts Club began its life in the Waverley Temperance Hotel, which one rather suspects represented Glasgow at its most dourly Protestant. In these early years it was less a "gentlemen's club" in the developed sense and more of an association of artists who met to compare and criticise each other's work. Art criticism is a famously thirsty business, and soon the membership hankered after a more refreshing selection of beverages than were served in the Waverley. Several other premises were occupied before the club moved into its present digs on Bath Street.

Once the Glasgow Arts Club was settled it began to attract a bohemian clientele. Preeminent amongst these early members was R.B. Cunninghame Graham, founder of both the Scottish Labour Party and what become the Scottish National Party (of which he was also the first president), and therefore a man with much to answer for. An accomplished horseman, Cunninghame Graham spent some time as a South American gaucho, where he was press-ganged into a revolutionary army following an unsuccessful spell as a cattle rancher. During his South American sojourn Cunninghame Graham befriended Buffalo Bill, who later visited the Glasgow Arts Club, much to the amusement and delight of the membership.[67] "Don Roberto", as he was known in South America, died in 1936 at Buenos Aires and is buried in a ruined Augustinian Priory on the tiny island of Inchmahome.

The clubhouse of the Glasgow Arts Club is itself a work of art. Opened in 1893 it is a perfect expression of what came to be known as the Glasgow School, containing early work by one of its preeminent practitioners: Charles Rennie Mackintosh. Mackintosh was only twenty-five when he was employed as a draughtsman by the architect John Keppie, already a member of the club, to help convert two houses on Bath Street into a suitable clubhouse. For over a century the whole scheme was credited to Keppie, but it is now recognised that Mackintosh was responsible for sections of the interior. Mackintosh's hand can be detected in the club's noble gallery, which – incidentally – one does not have to be a member in order to visit. The gallery is dominated by a frieze of delicate greens and pinks in a swirling Art Nouveau design crowned with thistles. It is the sort of piece

[67] William Frederick "Buffalo Bill" Cody spent four months in Glasgow from November 1891 and February 1892, headlining a sell-out show also featuring Annie Oakley and three Sioux Indians. He returned to Scotland in 1901 when he climbed Edinburgh's Calton Hill (see previous chapter) and exclaimed "ain't she a beaut!"

which inspires strong feelings; I happen to think that it is *marvellous*.

Recently restored to an approximation of Mackintosh's original design, the frieze has gained some notoriety as one of the artist's earliest extant works. There are several less conspicuous examples of Mackintosh's handiwork which also deserve a closer look. Mackintosh's influence may be seen in the ventilation covers and lettering around the fireplace in the gallery, but loveliest of all are a pair of polished brass finger plates, which demonstrate Mackintosh's early move away from stolid Scottish baronial to a restrained and sensual *Japonisme*.

A prosperous trading city, Glasgow's shipyards on the River Clyde benefitted from Japan's decision in the 1890s to open itself up to intercourse with the West. Mackintosh collected the Japanese architectural books and prints which landed in Glasgow's shipyards, and found much to admire in their clean lines and creative use of natural imagery. Like all great artists he nicked the best bits and used them in his own work. Both finger plates in the Glasgow Arts Club feature a stylised floral design typical of the restrained Glasgow Art Nouveau. On one of the plates the bulbous head of a plant is supported by an elegant female form, lithe of limb and pert of bosom, arms upstretched and head tilted coquettishly. It is a design beautiful in its restraint. The plates are fixed on the main doors to the gallery and offer a foretaste of the grander treasures which lie within.

Mackintosh became the one of the most important Scottish architects of the twentieth century, and his ideas on design influenced a generation of British artists. In the Glasgow Arts Club one can see the first budding of this genius. Like many artists, Mackintosh had his share of unhappiness. In 1915 he was arrested on suspicion of being a German spy whilst on holiday in Suffolk. Some neighbours apparently mistook Mackintosh's Glaswegian accent for German and reported him to the military, who attempted an arrest. Sometimes it is easy to see why the Scottish so despise their southern neighbours.

BIBLIOGRAPHY

CLUBLAND (GENERAL)

Bernard Darwin, *British Clubs* (1943)

Jolee Edmondson, "Old Boys' Clubs" in *Cigar Aficionado* (March/April 1997)

Tom Girtin, *The Abominable Clubman* (1964)

Charles Graves, *Leather Armchairs: The Chivas Regal Book of London Clubs* (1963)

Arthur Griffiths, *Clubs and Clubmen* (1907)

Joseph Hatton, *Clubland: London and Provincial* (1890)

Stephen Hoare, *Palaces of Power: The Birth and Evolution of London's Clubland* (2019)

Anthony Lejeune & Malcolm Lewis, *The Gentlemen's Clubs of London* (1979)

Trustees of the Cartoon Museum, *Cartoons from Private London Clubs: A Peep into Clubland* (2009)

Jack Malvern, "Inside the Secretive World of Gentlemen's Clubs" in *The Times* (29th June 2012)

Ralph Nevill, *London Clubs: Their History and Treasures* (1911)

David Palfreyman, *London's Pall Mall Clubs* (2019)

INDIVIDUAL CLUBS

(Alphabetically, by club)

Anthony Dixon, *The Army & Navy Club 1837-2008* (2009)

C.W. Firebrace, *The Army & Navy Club: 1837-1933* (1933)

F.R.Cowell, *The Athenaeum, Club and Social Life in London 1824-1974* (1975)

Richard Walker, "The Athenaeum Collection" and Bryan Bennett, "The Athenaeum Question Book" in The Athenaeum Club, *Armchair Athenians: Essays From The Athenaeum* (2001)

Roger Fulford, *Boodle's 1762-1962: A Short History* (1962)

Philip Ziegler and Desmond Seward, *Brooks's: A Social History* (1991)

Jan Coughtrie, *The Caledonian Club Collection: A History of the Club and its Collection of Art and Artefacts* (2014)

Andrew Hignell, *Always Amongst Friends: The Cardiff and County Club 1866-2016* (2017)

Graham Redcliffe, *One Hundred Not Out... The City Livery Club 1914- 2014* (2014)

Bruce Redford, *Dilettanti: The Antic and the Antique in Eighteenth-Century England* (2008)

Charlie Jacoby, *The East India Club: A History* (2009)

Andrew Herd, *The Flyfishers: A History of the Flyfishers' Club* (2019)

John Morgan, "Curator's Report'" in *The Flyfishers Journal* (Summer, 2014)

Geoffrey Wansell, *The Garrick Club: A History* (2004)

David Cuppelditch, *The London Sketch Club* (1994)

Tim Newark, *The In & Out: A History of the Naval and Military Club* (2015)

Roy Cowell, *A History of the Nottingham Club* (2014)

Hugh Riches, *A History of the Oriental Club* (1998)

Craig McDonald, Alex Fulluck, & Amy Crangle, *Recipes From the Reform: A Selection of Recipes from the Reform Club, London* (2014)

Piers Brendon, *The Motoring Century: Story of the Royal Automobile Club* (1997)

The RAC, *The Motor House, Woodcote Park* (2016)

Captain A.R. Ward, *The Chronicles of the Royal Thames Yacht Club* (1999)

Aaron Watson, *The Savage Club* (1907)

Percy Bradshaw, *Brother Savages and Guests* (1958)

Matthew Norgate & Alan Wykes, *Not so Savage* (1976)

Garrett Anderson, *Hang Your Halo in the Hall: A History of the Savile Club* (1993)

The Savile Club Sesquicentennial Series:

- ~ Ken Allen & Robert J.D. Harding, *The Savile Club Scientists* (2019)
- ~ Michael Bloch, *Guide to the Savile Monument* (2018)
- ~ Robert J.D. Harding, *Suggestions' Books: A Selection of Entries 1868-1968* (2018)
- ~ Robert J.D. Harding, *A Sesquicentennial Miscellany* (2019)

John Martin Robinson, *The Travellers Club: A Bicentennial History: 1819-2019* (2019)

George Chambers & William Roulston (eds.), *The Ulster Reform Club Past and Present* (2009)

Evelyn Haselgrove, *University Women's Club: A History* (1994)

Anthony Lejeune, *White's: The First Three Hundred Years* (1993)

Evelyn Ackerman, "Costume is the Key: Seventeenth Century Miniature Portraits with Costume Overlays" in *Dress: The Journal of the Costume Society of America* 34.1

Clive Aslet, *An Exuberant Catalogue of Dreams: The Americans Who Revived the Country House in Britain* (2013)

Naim Attallah, *A Scribbler in Soho: A Celebration of Auberon Waugh* (2019)

Henry Howarth Bashford, *Augustus Carp, Esq. by Himself: Being the Autobiography of a Really Good Man* (1924)

Max Beerbohm, *Zuleika Dobson* (1911)

Percy V. Bradshaw, *Drawn From Memory* (1943)

Alistair Cooke, *A Gift from the Churchills: The Primrose League 1883–2004* (2010)

Ruth Cowen, *Relish: The Extraordinary Life of Alexis Soyer, Victorian Celebrity Chef* (2006)

Bernard Darwin, "Some Curious Wagers" in *The Strand Magazine* (1910)

Charles Darwin, *The Expression of the Emotions in Man and Animals* (1872)

Robert Edgerton, *Africa's Armies: From Honor To Infamy* (2008)

Lord Frederic Hamilton, *The Vanished Pomps of Yesterday: Being Some Random Reminiscences of a British Diplomat* (1920)

Christopher Howse, *Soho in the Eighties* (2018)

Robert Rhodes James (ed.), *"Chips": The Diaries of Chips Channon* (1967)

Neil Jenkins, *John Beard: Handel and Garrick's Favourite Tenor* (2012)

Giuseppe Tomasi di Lampedusa, *The Leopard* (1958)

Laurie Lee, *Cider with Rosie* (1959)

Sam Leith, "The Artist Formerly Known as Whistler" in *The Spectator* (22nd February 2014)

George MacDonald Fraser, *Royal Flash* (1970)

Robert Machray, *The Night Side of London* (1902)

David Meredith (ed.), *Kyffin dan Sylw/Kyffin in View* (2018)

Alexander Norwich Tayler, *The Book of the Duffs* (1914)

~ Jessica Martin, "Walton, Izaak"

~ Richard A. Storey, "Simms, Frederick Richard"

Steven Parissien, *Adam Style* (1996)

Alexander Pope, *Moral Essays, Ep. I* (1731)

J.R. Robinson, *"Old Q": A Memoir of William Douglas, Fourth Duke of Queensberry, K.T., One of "the Fathers of the Turf," with a Full Account of His Celebrated Matches and Wagers, Etc.* (1895)

Anthony Sampson, *Anatomy of Modern Britain* (1965)

Ronald Storrs, *Orientations* (1943)

Witold Szablowski, *How to Feed a Dictator* (2020)

Damien Thompson, *Loose Canon: A Portrait of Brian Brindley* (2004)

Adrian Tinniswood, *The Long Weekend: Life in the English Country House Between the Wars* (2016)

"Woollen Laws" in *Notes and Queries* 5.*vi* (9th September, 1876)

WEB PAGES

https://www.awatrees.com/2014/10/09/disraeli-gladstone-arboriculture/

http://www.britishpigs.org.uk/trad1.htm

https://www.cityoflondon.gov.uk/things-to-do/london-metropolitan-archives/the-collections/Pages/water-supply.aspx

https://colinsmythe.co.uk/charles-elme-francatelli-crockfords-and-the-royal-connection/

https://www.countrylife.co.uk/country-life/in-praise-of-porkers-7-native-british-pig-breeds-82781

https://www.gracesguide.co.uk/William_Fisher_Hobbs

https://www.harrogateadvertiser.co.uk/news/people/restoring-harrogate-s-mysterious-the-club-that-sherlock-holmes-creator-loved-1-7827141

http://www.historyhouse.co.uk/articles/buried_in_wool.html

INDEX

INDEX OF CLUBS

*Denotes defunct club
†Denotes fictional club
(Denotes footnote)

GENERAL INDEX

Printed in Great Britain
by Amazon

29859221R00160